TRUE HOPE DARKEST HOUR

BY

PASTOR ERIC SANCHEZ

DORRANCE PUBLISHING CO
EST. 1920
PITTSBURGH, PENNSYLVANIA 15238

Dorrance Publishing Co
585 Alpha Drive
Pittsburgh, PA 15238
Visit our website at www.dorrancebookstore.com

ISBN: 978-1-6453-0985-2
eISBN: 978-1-6461-0274-7

DEDICATION

For all of the Christian volunteers who risk their lives to minister God's love, mercy, forgiveness, and redemption every time they enter a correctional facility.

ACKNOWLEDGEMENTS

This work could not have been possible without the cooperation of the New Mexico Attorney General's Office. They provided the author with a copy of the Report of the Attorney General on the February 2nd and 3rd, 1980 Riot at the Penitentiary of New Mexico, dated June 5th, 1980. This report outlined the conditions of the penitentiary, the riot, and the aftermath of the riot.

I would also like to thank my friends, Larry Lucero, former New Mexico State University professor, and Theresa Tafoya, former administrator with the New Mexico Environment Department. These two were instrumental in helping me with the editing, formatting, and content of this book.

Above all, I thank my wife, Karen, for her patience and support as this work was being conceived and completed.

PREFACE

The following story is a work of fiction but is based on an actual historical event. On February 2nd and 3rd, 1980, a group of hardened criminals, inmates at the New Mexico State Penitentiary south of Santa Fe, took control of the prison. The ensuing riot lasted 36 hours and resulted in the murders of 33 inmates. The murders were committed by other inmates, primarily the hardcore element of the prison population, many of whom were serving life sentences.

The riot of February 2nd and 3rd, 1980 at the New Mexico State Penitentiary was, up to that time, the most violent prison riot in the history of the American Correctional System. A May 26th, 2011 documentary film on the riot by the British Broadcasting Corporation (BBC) included this statement: "All the forces of hell were unleashed, and it happened right there."

The terms referred to in the novel, such as, "The belly of the beast," were real aspects of the penitentiary. "The belly of the beast" referred to a sensory-deprivation chamber that was used by penitentiary officials as punishment for rules infractions by inmates.

"The snitch jacket" was the way correction officers administered the day-to-day operations of the prison. They used inmates to inform on other inmates. If an inmate refused to cooperate with prison officials, they were threatened with having the label of "snitch" hung on them. If that occurred and an inmate was wearing a "snitch jacket," that inmate's life was forfeit. The other inmates would take their revenge on the informant, whether the inmate had cooperated or not.

For their own protection, "snitches" were placed in a separate cellblock called protective custody. These inmates become the primary targets of the hardcore rioters who took over the prison.

In the novel, the main character, Jesus (Hay-SOOS) De La Cruz loses his young mother and is raised by his religious grandmother to love God. Through their poverty and despite extreme circumstances, God prepares Hay-SOOS for a calling that he never expected to fulfill.

Hay-SOOS finds himself serving time in prison as the result of a false accusation and encounters the hardships of prison life. During his time in prison, however, he finds God and is redeemed by the blood of Jesus Christ. His life is transformed from that day on.

As he serves his time and following his release, Hay-SOOS embarks on a journey at once terrifying and rewarding; one that will test his love and obedience to God beyond anything he ever imagined.

Who would have thought Hay-SOOS would choose to return to prison?

INSPIRATION FOR THE STORY

I started in prison ministry in 2005 and have been in prison ministry for over 14 years. I always felt that I could do much more for the Lord, using all the talents and gifts He had given me. In the past, I had created a children's TV program for TV32 a Christian television station. With their parent's permission, I had interviewed children in shopping malls and tied the interviews in with New Mexico statistics on child abuse. I knew there was a creative part in me, but I had never thought of writing a novel. One night the Lord spoke to my spirit and gave me the desire to create a story about Christian volunteers and the prison ministries, and how they are making a huge impact in the correctional system. This is how the idea came to me about using the 1980 riot that took place at the New Mexico State Penitentiary as the setting for the story.

Psalm 139:7, 8 says, "Where can I go from Thy Spirit? Or where can I flee from thy presence? If I ascend into heaven, thou are there. If I make my bed in hell, behold, Thou art there." There was a quote from the documentary done by the BBC: "All the forces of hell were unleashed, and it happen right there." Psalm 139: 7, 8 indicates that where the forces of hell were present, the Spirit of the Living God was also there. This novel presents the truth of the Word of God, "…greater is He who is in you, than he who is in the world."

Even though the Word of God is true, the names of the characters in this book are fictional and are the product of the author's imagination. Any resemblance to actual persons, living or dead is entirely coincidental.

Pastor Eric Sanchez

REVIEW

Eric Sanchez, being inspired by an incredible true story, takes us into the experiences of a young man coming to faith in Christ, his run in with the law, and a guilty charge that lands him in prison. We follow his story and his struggle to prove his innocence. I found myself inspired and the narrative gripping as well as emotionally moving as I followed the young man though his experiences and challenges. This story kept me absorbed, eager to read more, to discover what the next turn of events would bring about for Jesus (Hay-SOOS). This short story packs a punch that is not easily forgotten. Eric shows exceptional promise as an author and I look forward to reading more of his work in the future.

Eric Lamb
Pastor of Calvary Church,
Albuquerque New Mexico

ABOUT THE AUTHOR

Eric Sanchez was born in Las Vegas, NM and for a short time lived in Santa Rosa, NM. In 1948, his family moved to Albuquerque where he was raised and now resides with his wife, Karen. At the age of 36, he became a Christian. He has been sales manager for KNKT 107.1, a local Christian radio station. He has created and produced TV programs for a Local Christian television station, including "Kids' Point of View," 30-minute interviews with children. The Lord called him into prison ministry in 2005 where he still serves today. He has ministered in federal halfway houses, state and privately-operated prisons in New Mexico. He was ordained as a pastor in a prison in 2008. True Hope Fellowship church was formed and named by the inmates at a state prison. He was asked to pastor the church. He is the owner and CEO of the Landscape and Sprinkler Company LLC. In his company, he hires ex-felons as an extension of his prison ministry. He provides on-the-job training, teaching the employees the trade of irrigation technician and the basic skills of landscaping.

TRUE HOPE DARKEST HOUR

PROLOGUE

Hello, my name is Hay-SOOS, which is the Spanish name for Jesus. My last name is De La Cruz, which is my Grandma's maiden name. In English, HAY-SOOS DE LA CRUZ means "JESUS OF THE CROSS." This is the name given to me by my grandma at birth.

This is my life's story; the events that occurred before and leading up to the prison riot at the Penitentiary of New Mexico just south of Santa Fe in 1980. I experienced a calling that I never thought God would put on my life, one that I never ever expected would happen to me. Where do I start? I suppose the best place is at the very beginning.

CHAPTER ONE

RECONCILIATION

It was a dark, dreary, cold, and wet morning in Santa Fe, New Mexico on Christmas Eve at 2:00 am when my mother, Rosa, reluctantly called her mother, my grandmother, Mama Luz. She called her to tell her that she was going into labor at Christus St. Vincent Medical Center, ready to give birth to me.

At the young age of 17, my mother Rosa became pregnant when she was given too much to drink at a neighbor's party, got drunk, and was gang- raped. Months later when she finally got the nerve to tell Mama Luz that she was pregnant and didn't know who the father was, my grandma became furious. She told her to leave and ordered my mother out of her house.

My grandmother is a very religious lady of 70 years of age. She was raised in a very religious Roman Catholic family and was the youngest of three girls. At an early age, her two sisters joined the Roman Catholic Sisters of Loretto, taking the vows of obedience, chastity, and poverty. My grandmother would have done the same, except for the fact that she got pregnant out of wedlock with my mother Rosa when she was 17 years of age. Her life was that of raising Rosa, her daughter. She always resented the fact that she was never able to become a nun like her sisters. She named her daughter Rosa after her middle sister, whom she admired the most and who took the name of Sister Rosa when she joined the Sisters of Loretto. This is why my grandmother took it so hard when she found out that her daughter had taken the same path as her. She would not live under the same roof with a daughter who had committed such a heinous sin, even though she had done the same. Her resentment all those years for not being able to become a nun was taken out on my mother when she told her to leave the house.

My mother Rosa moved out and went to live with other family members, and a few times on the streets of Santa Fe, to survive during the nine months of her pregnancy.

My grandma, after receiving my mother's call and feeling guilty for having made my mother move out, was overjoyed to hear her voice. She realized by the sound of her voice that there was something desperately wrong.

"Please hurry, Mama, I don't have much time."

My grandma rushed to the hospital to be with my mother Rosa. Just as she arrived at the hospital and was walking into the delivery room, a doctor pulled my grandma Mama Luz aside to tell her that her daughter Rosa was in serious trouble with complications and that she wouldn't survive the birth of her baby boy. The doctor told her they would be able to save the baby but not the mother and that the baby would be healthy and strong. My grandma rushed to my mom's bedside to be with her. With my mother's last dying breath, she whispered to my grandmother that she was so sorry for what had happened and asked for forgiveness. As she was speaking, my grandmother was holding her with tears in her eyes and told her that she loved her and had forgiven her. In her last dying breath, she looked into my grandmother's eyes and said, "Please, Mama, take care of my son; raise him to be just like you, knowing and loving God. Ask God to watch over him, keep him safe, and use him some day to do good."

My grandma, in her broken crying voice and a broken heart, promised that she would. With that said, my mother Rosa passed away in my grandma's arms.

 Pastor Eric Sanchez

CHAPTER TWO

MY FIRST
TWELVE YEARS

After the passing of my mother, my grandma Mama Luz was given custody of me. She raised me as if I was her own son. The first thing she did was to have me baptized with the name of Jesus (Hay-SOOS) De La Cruz. I was eight-years-old when she enrolled me at the Loretto Academy Catholic School. With the help of her two sisters who had become nuns, she raised me in the Roman Catholic Church.

I received my first holy communion at the age of eight and was confirmed in the church at the age of 12. I had to attend Mass every day and especially on Sunday. I just went along with the program. I sometimes thought they were grooming me to become a priest.

My grandma, whom I now called Mama Luz and considered my mother, lived in a small three-room house next to the priest's rectory, which was close to the Loretto Academy and Loretto Chapel. Mama Luz was hired to cook for the priests and do their daily cleaning. That was how she made a living to support us, but still, it was not enough to live on. I remember the late nights that she stayed up baking biscochitos, empanadas, and sometimes cooking tamales. The aroma of the kitchen was heavenly. She would always ask me, "Mi hijo, how does that taste? Do I need more cinnamon on the biscochitos? Do the tamales taste too hot?"

I was the one who tasted everything. No wonder I was a fat little kid. I would always tell Mama Luz, "You are the greatest cook in the whole wide world, muy delicioso." After school I would rush home to load up with all that was baked the night before. I would ride my bike around the plaza selling the tamales, biscochitos, and empanadas. It only took a few hours before all that was baked at night was sold. I was so excited to tell Mama Luz that I had sold all the food and how much money we had made. She would always say to me, "Thank you, mi hijo. You are the greatest salesman in the whole wide world." She would give me a few dollars. I always felt safe and loved by Mama Luz and I loved her with all my heart. She was my life and I became her life. These were the happiest days of my young life. I loved that she was very over-shadowing and protective of me.

On the other hand, my two aunts who were nuns were quite different. They spoiled me. I remember when I would go visit them how they would take me to a Chapel called Loretto Chapel. Next to teaching at the Academy, they were also responsible for keeping the chapel clean and what they called "The Miraculous Staircase" polished. I would ask my aunt, Sister Rosa, "Why do you call the stairs 'Miraculous Staircase?'" Sister Rosa would sit me down and for hours tell me the legend of the Staircase. She would tell me that after the chapel was complete, there was no way to access the upper loft. Carpenters were called in to address the problem but had no answers. So, the sisters prayed a novena to St Joseph, the patron saint of carpenters.

On the ninth and final day of prayer, on a bitter cold late night, a stranger knocked on the door of the convent. One of the sisters came to the door to see who was there. As she opened the door, there stood a man with a donkey at his side. He was dressed in a tunic with long gray hair and a gray beard and was wearing sandals, not dressed for bitter cold weather. He had a small satchel draped over his shoulder with a few tools inside the satchel. He was inquiring if there was any work available. He said he

    Pastor Eric Sanchez

would work for food and a place to sleep. The sisters kindly invited him in and gave him something to eat. The sisters shared the dilemma they were faced with about the staircase to the upper loft. The stranger told the sisters that he was a carpenter by trade and offered to build the staircase for the chapel in exchange of meals and lodging. He told the sisters that it would take about six months to build. So, the sisters knew that he was the answer to their prayers and agreed to hire him.

Sister Rosa would always point out the Three Mysteries that still surround the spiral staircase: the identity of its builder, the type of wood used, and the physics of its construction. As he said, it took him exactly six months to build it, with two 360-degree turns and no visible means of support. To this day, engineers still cannot figure out how he built the staircase.

"When the circular staircase was completed, the carpenter disappeared without pay or thanks. No one knew his name or where he came from. We sisters believe that he was St. Joseph the carpenter, the foster father of Jesus, and that God sent him to build the staircase."

My aunt Sister Rosa loved telling me the same story over and over again. Not wanting to hurt her feelings, I would listen to her as if it was the first time I had heard it. I always acted so excited to hear it and ask her, "Sister Rosa, is that what you call a miracle?"

She would answer, "Yes, Hay-SOOS. It was a miracle and that is why you should always pray to God when you need help. God always helps you when you pray to Him."

"I will, Aunt Rosa. I will." I loved her so much. She was so loving and good to me.

CHAPTER THREE

LOOKING BACK

I realized how blessed I was to have my grandma, Mama Luz, raise me. After going through grade school, middle school, and finally graduating high school at Loretto Academy, I remember all the friends that I had made.

One particular teacher at the Academy with whom I became very close was a young priest, Father Javier Ortiz, who taught catechism class. He singled me out as one of his favorite students. When he would ask the class questions about God and no one would raise their hand, he would always call on me. I would always have the right answer. He would ask me if I ever thought of becoming a priest. I would say, "I'm not good enough to be a priest."

He would say, "Start working on it, Hay-SOOS."

He encouraged me to sign up for altar boy classes. Because of him, I was able to serve as an altar boy at the cathedral. I don't think our relationship was an accident. It came about because Mama Luz and I lived close to the priests' rectory. I began to look at him as my mentor.

On several late nights, I could hear noises of grinding, pounding, and welding coming from an old building next to the rectory. It was an old abandoned car garage, which was attached to the rectory. One Saturday morning on my way to serve Mass, I happened to ride by the garage and saw father Javier working in the garage. I pedaled up to the garage to see what he was doing and say hello.

"Good morning, Father. What are you doing?" I asked.

"Good morning to you, Hay-SOOS. I'm building a low-rider bike for a friend of mine. Someone stole his bike a few days ago."

"Wow, I didn't know you could build bikes!"

"Yep, before I became a priest, this was what I did for a hobby, to make a few bucks. It keeps me busy. You know, Jesus worked with his hands. He was a carpenter. He worked with wood and I work with metal. I love working with my hands."

"Father, would you look at my bike when you have some time? The front wheel wobbles a lot."

"Sure, Hay-SOOS, do you have time now?"

"I think so."

"Bring it here. Let's see why it wobbles."

As he started working on my bike, we started talking. He shared a lot about his life before becoming a priest. Looking into my eyes with his eyebrow raised, he said, "So, Hay-SOOS, tell me about what's been going on in your life. I haven't seen you since you graduated from the academy."

I shared with Father that I lived with my grandma in the house next to the rectory.

"Mama Luz De La Cruz lives in that house."

"Don't tell me that's your grandma."

"Yes, that's my grandma. Where do you know my grandma from?"

"Everyone knows Mama Luz. She's the best cook in Santa Fe. She does the cooking and cleaning at the rectory. She is like a mother to me. I never knew my mother. Not too many people know that I was raised in an orphanage. I pray that she will be with us for many more years. As you know, it's difficult for her to walk and get around like she used to. I don't know what the rectory would do without her. Has Mama Luz always lived here in Santa Fe?"

    Pastor Eric Sanchez

"Yes, all her life. She was raised just a few blocks from the academy."

"So, who is your real mother?"

"My real mother was Rosa. She was Mama Luz's daughter."

"Where is your mom now?"

"My mom died giving birth to me."

"So, Rosa De La Cruz is your mother,"

"Yes, that's my mother."

Father stayed silent for a minute, like he was in deep thought.

"Wow, Hay-SOOS! When I was in high school, I knew a girl in my cat-echism class named Rosa and her last name was De La Cruz. Could she have been your mom?"

"I don't know, maybe."

"Rosa was pretty, smart, and fun to be around. We enjoyed each other's company and became friends. In fact, her locker was next to mine. What a small world!"

"Are you sure, Father Javier?"

"Who else could it be? Rosa told me she never knew her father. For some reason, her mother pulled her out of school in her senior year. I never knew why or what happened to her. I never saw her again. Your mother was a very beautiful lady. I am so sorry to hear about your mom's passing. She's in heaven looking down and watching over you for sure."

"I hope so."

After sharing some of our life stories, Father had fixed my bike from wobbling. I thanked him for fixing my bike and sharing about my mom. It was a lot to ponder over. I pondered whether Father Javier could possibly be my father, wishful thinking. I forgot about it and biked on to serve Mass.

Ever since that day, Father Javier became my best friend. We worked together on bicycles of all kinds. He taught me everything there is to know about repairing and building bikes. I took up the hobby and built a real nice low-rider bike for myself.

I loved showing off my bike. There's a park with a nice playground for kids not far from the Academy. On Saturdays the park is crowded with children playing. My friends would meet there to hang out. Of course, that's where I would ride to show off my really cool bike. It didn't take long before some of the guys became my friends and would come over to check out my bike. Some would ask if they could ride it around the park. Others would ask me who built it. I would stick out my chest and say, "I built it. Father Javier taught me how to repair and build bikes. That's his hobby."

A few of my close friends asked if I would help them build a bike. "Sure," I said. "Father Javier told me that it would be ok if I ever wanted to use the garage and his tools to build bikes for myself or to help others with their repairs."

On that day, I made a lot of new friends. They started calling me "the bike whisperer." Everyone wanted to be my friend. I have to admit it was great being the talk of the park and popular with the girls. Life couldn't get any better than this.

A week later after serving Mass for Father Javier, he called me to his chambers. "Hay-SOOS, what is this that I hear that you are now called 'the bike whisperer?' Are you bragging about your bike?"

"No, Father. Well, somewhat. I was excited to ride my bike to the park to show it off."

"So, you were bragging,"

"I wouldn't say I was bragging, just very proud of my bike. Is pride a bad thing?"

"Hay-SOOS, what was the scripture reading at Mass last Sunday?"

"Sorry, Father. I don't remember."

"I read out of the book of Proverbs 16:18-19."

"Oh, now I remember. You said that pride goes before destruction and a haughty spirit before a fall. That it's better to be of a humble spirit than of a proud spirit."

"What was my sermon about?"

"Something about ego."

"At least you got that right. Ego is what God bred into man to stir up his natural desires, motivations, and attitudes. Man's ego makes him want

 Pastor Eric Sanchez

to take initiative, be the leader, provider, and protector of his family. You took the initiative to learn about bike building. Now you have that knowledge. Have you ever wanted to protect someone you love, a friend or a family member?"

"Yes, my grandma. I won't let anyone hurt her!"

"See? That feeling inside you is your ego working, Hay-SOOS."

"Really? That's my ego working? Father, I have this recurring dream that someday I am going to save someone's life."

"That may be true. God shows and speaks to us in dreams. Hay-SOOS, you are to have a humbler spirit. A proud look and a lying tongue are an abomination unto God. Always remember that."

"Thanks, Father, for sharing that with me."

I remember Father Javier once said to me, "Hay-SOOS, one day can change the rest of your life." I really didn't understand what he meant at the time. But now I do. In my wildest dreams, I never thought this would ever happen to me on that late Saturday evening. What I am about to share with you now did change the rest of my life. Why would God do this to me?

CHAPTER FOUR

NINE YEARS LATER

It was a cool autumn evening. The sun was starting to set. It had been a fun-filled afternoon, showing off my low-rider bike, letting the girls ride the bike, shooting some hoops and hanging out with my friends. It was getting late and everyone was starting to leave. I headed home, exhausted and hungry. Walking through the front door, the aroma of fresh cooked tamales hit me. Mama Luz, hearing the front door closing, yelled out, "Is that you, mi hijo?"

"Yes, Mama Luz, it's me."

"Come sit and have some tamales."

As I started towards the kitchen, I remembered I left my jacket on the stone wall at the park. I yelled at my grandma, "I'll be right back!"

"Where are you going?" she asked. "You just got home!"

"I left my jacket at the park. I need to go get it before someone takes it. That's my only jacket."

"Don't be long!" she yelled out.

"I won't," I called out.

I was pedaling as fast as I could, thinking to myself, "I hope no one has taken my jacket." When I got to the park and saw my jacket, I was so relieved. But then I noticed a young girl still waiting for someone to pick her up. She looked a little afraid and anxious. She was around 12-years-old. I started to walk over to see if I could sit with her until someone came for her. Then there appeared an older man walking towards her. I thought to myself, "He must be her father." So, I proceeded to leave. As I turned to leave, the little girl started screaming, "Stop it! Leave me alone! Don't touch me! Get away from me! You're hurting me! Help! Help!" I turned back to help but froze in my tracks. I then saw what this man was doing to her. He had his hand over her mouth and was raising her dress over her face. She was struggling but to no avail. He was just too strong. I couldn't believe what I was seeing. I couldn't move. I yelled out, "God! Help her!"

When he finished with her, he pulled out a knife and started to slit her throat. I yelled out, "Stop, don't do that!" When he heard and saw me, he dropped his knife and ran off.

The little girl just lay there, cut, shaking and crying. I ran over to help to see if she was ok. She didn't respond. She just looked at me, crying, with fear on her face. I kept asking her, "Are you ok? Are you ok?" I didn't know how to help. I felt so helpless. As I stood over the girl trying to help, I noticed a police car patrolling the park. I frantically waved and yelled, "Help, help! Over here, over here!"

They saw me and ran over to where we were. They looked at me with contempt in their eyes. One of the officers grabbed me while the other officer bent over to help the girl.

"What's your name?" When she didn't respond, the officer kept telling her, "You're safe now; we're here to help you. Tell me what happened."

The girl, looking up at him and still shaking and crying, said, "A man raised my dress over my face and hurt me." The officer looked up at me and then looked at the girl and asked her, "Is this the man who did this to you?"

The girl, looking up at me, said, "Yes."

"That's not true, officer. I would never do anything like this. I can't believe she said it was me." As I tried to explain to the officers what I saw, the officers were handcuffing me and putting me in their vehicle. "Officer, I'm telling you the truth. It wasn't me. It was someone else who did this."

"You just watched and did nothing?"

"I was afraid and froze."

"You sorry, SOB! How could you just watch and do nothing!"

My head hung low and I felt ashamed of myself. They told me, "You are under arrest for the rape of a minor."

"No, no, that's not true. Where are you taking me? I need to call my grandma."

"You're not calling anyone. You're going to the county detention center. You are allowed one call and can call your grandma from there."

I prayed all the way, "God, why are you doing this to me, why? I can't believe this is happening! Please, God, tell them I didn't do this! Don't let me go to jail!"

At the detention center, they booked me and made me remove all my clothing and made me put on a yellow shirt and pants. They said I could make one call. Since my grandma didn't have a phone at the house, I called the rectory and asked for Father Javier. It was Father Javier who answered. I was in tears.

"This is Hay-SOOS, Father. Something terrible has happened!"

"Are you ok? Where are you calling from?"

"I'm calling from the Santa Fe County Detention Center."

"What are you doing there?"

"It's a long story, but can you go get my grandma, so I can talk to her?"

"She came by the rectory asking if I had seen you or knew where you were. She said you should have been home hours ago. She is worried about you."

"I need to tell her I didn't do it,"

"Didn't do what?"

"Please, can you just go get her?"

"Ok, ok, I'll have her call you back. Tell me what you didn't do."

"Sorry, Father, but my time is up. I have to hang up now."

After I hung up, I was led down a corridor to a holding cell. It was dark and gloomy and smelled like urine and sweat. Some of the men were drunk. Others were passed out on the floor. I couldn't believe I was in this place. I just went to a corner of the cell to sit and hide, praying no one would bother me.

I never got a call back from my grandma that night. The next morning, my grandma and Father Javier were at the front office waiting to see me. The guard came for me and took me to the visitation room where they were both waiting. The guards put shackles on my feet and hands. I looked like a convict. I was behind a glass shield. I spoke to my grandmother on a phone on the other side of the glass.

"Te quiero, hijo mio! Que has hecho? I love you, my son, what have you done?"

"Grandma, I haven't done anything,"

Father Javier grabbed the phone.

"Hay-SOOS! What happened? What have you not done?"

I shared with them what had happened in detail. In tears, my grandma dropped to the floor in shock. Two guards helped lift her off the floor and took her back to the front office to attend to her. Father Javier was right at her side the whole time.

At the front office, Father Javier noticed Officer Flores, one of the arresting officers, writing his report. Officer Flores attends Father Javier's Mass every Sunday. The officer, seeing Father Javier, walked over and asked him what he was doing at the jail. Father shared with him about Hay-SOOS and his relationship with him. Officer Flores asked Father Javier, "Is this the same boy who serves as an altar boy during your Mass?"

"Yes, he is. He has served Mass for me for many years."

"Father, I am sorry to tell you this, but your boy Hay-SOOS has serious charges facing him."

Father asked him, "What charges?"

Officer Flores replied, "Violation of a minor, described as rape, and possible attempted murder. He could be facing a prison sentence of 25 years to life if found guilty."

Father Javier lowered his head and nodded, "I can't believe this has

     Pastor Eric Sanchez

happened. I know in my heart Hay-SOOS didn't do it. It's not in him to do something like that."

Officer Flores put his hand on Father's shoulder to console him, "Sorry, Father. I wish I didn't have to do this. I pray he's not found guilty."

"Thanks, Officer Flores. You were just doing your job."

Father Javier walked over to where my grandma was resting.

"How are you doing, Mama Luz? Can you stand up?"

"Yes, Father. Get me out of this horrible place."

Father Javier made sure that Mama Luz got home ok.

As I was removed from the visitation room, the guards walked me back to a different part of the jail. Walking down the hall, I noticed each cell had one person inside. Curious, I asked the guards, "Why is there only one person inside each cell?"

"This is 'the hole,' solitary confinement. It's for your own protection."

I asked them, "Why?"

He said, "Because of the charge pending against you."

"What charge?"

"Rape of a minor"

"WHAT! I NEVER RAPED ANYONE. I didn't rape that girl!"

"That's the charge, kid. If we put you in a general pod with other inmates and they find out what you did, you're a dead man. Inmates hate snitches and child molesters and they will hurt you. The gay inmates will want to rape you, so here you are. You'll get used to it. It's nice and quiet, three meals a day, and at night, you get to go outside for one hour of recreation." Taking off the shackles, they said, "You'll be ok, kid."

"How long will I be here, officer?"

"Until you go before a judge," answered another officer.

"How long is that?"

"Don't know, could be a few weeks."

With that being said, they shut and locked the door. I was left in a cold, dark, 6'x12' cell with just my thoughts. I was reminded of what Father Javier once said to me. "One day can change the rest of your life." Today was that day. My life would never be the same. How I wish I had never gone to the park this morning! This is a bad dream and I want to wake up! Sister Rosa came to mind with the miracle of the staircase, that whenever I am in need of help, always pray to God and He will answer you. I fell to my knees in prayer and prayed the Our Father. I cried out to God, "Please help me! You know I didn't do this! I need a miracle right now! Amen."

Pastor Eric Sanchez

CHAPTER FIVE

BAIL

One week later, two guards came to my cell and said I had two visitors waiting in the visitation room. They put my hands and feet in shackles and walked me to the visitation room. It was Father Javier with another man I didn't know.

"Hello, Hay-SOOS," said Father Javier. "How are you doing?"

"Terrible, I hate this place. When am I going home? How is my grandma? Is she ok?"

"Sorry I haven't come to see you. I was told that you weren't allowed visitors. This is Robert Chavez. He's an attorney. Robert is going to represent you in court."

"Why? I haven't done anything wrong."

"That may be so, Hay-SOOS," said Mr. Chavez. "However, you are facing some very serious charges. Father Javier asked me to look at your file to see if I would be willing to represent you. Father and I go back a long time, we were raised in the same orphanage and he is like a brother to me. I told Father Javier that I am not a criminal defense attorney; this is not my field of expertise. Father said that no one else was willing to even review the case. In reviewing the case, I felt that you are innocent of the accusations against you and told Father Javier I am willing to represent you. With God's help, I will do my best. We go before Judge Gerald Gray in the morning at 9:00 a.m. I want to see about requesting bail for you until a trial date is set."

"What is bail?" I asked.

"It's letting you go home until a trial date is set."

"So, I'll be going home tomorrow?"

"Maybe, if the Judge approves it. He sets the amount of money if you do get bail. Someone needs to put up the money."

"I have $75 saved up."

"Hay-SOOS, it doesn't work that way. A bonding company usually puts up the money for you. You need to have collateral."

"What is that?"

"Something pledged as security for repayment of a loan."

"I have my bike."

"That's not going to work. We will cross that bridge when we get to it. Let's see what the Judge says tomorrow."

At daybreak the next morning, I was awakened by the banging on the door. "Hey, kid, it's breakfast time."

A food tray with bread, scrambled eggs, and a cup of cold coffee was being slipped through the small opening. The same breakfast I've forced myself to eat the last seven days. It was a far cry from the huevos rancheros my Grandma would fix for me in the morning. Finishing breakfast, I washed myself. Washing is throwing cold water on my face and using my shirt sleeve as a towel. I sat on the bed waiting for the marshal to escort me to the federal court house. I was tired of worrying, exhausted from lack of sleep, and hungry because the food is tasteless. "What if the Judge denies bail? What will my life be like if I go to prison? God, keep me from going to prison."

Hours later a marshal came and escorted me to a van. As I arrived at the court house, I was taken to the Judge's chamber where Father Javier and my attorney, Robert Chavez, were waiting. The marshal stood by the door.

   Pastor Eric Sanchez

"Good morning, Hay-SOOS. How are you?"

I just looked at them, shrugged my shoulders, and said, "Not good."

Father looked at me with a smile and said, "Today is a day that the Lord has made. You should rejoice and be glad in it."

I replied, "God has forsaken me."

My attorney turned to me and said, "Never lose hope. Judge Gray is an honest and fair judge."

Judge Gray entered the room. Glancing at me for a moment, he told us to be seated.

"Father Javier, it's nice to meet you, I've heard a lot about your community service in your parish."

"Thank you, Your Honor."

"Mr. Chavez, you represent the accused."

"Yes, Your Honor."

"Where is the prosecuting attorney, Mr. Allen?"

"Don't know, Your Honor."

Just then the prosecuting attorney walked in.

"Sorry I am late, Your Honor. I got stuck in traffic."

"This is a hearing for bail at the request of the defendant. Mr. Allen, state why you think bail should not be granted."

"Your Honor, the defendant is a young adult. Evidence will prove he is guilty of rape and attempted murder of a minor. He should be held without bail for the protection of the community. He would also be a flight risk. We can't have a rapist, especially a child rapist and killer, set free on the streets of Santa Fe to rape again."

"Mr. Chavez, state your defense."

"Your Honor, I have reviewed Mr. De La Cruz's file, and based on his background and the testimony of Father Javier, who has mentored Mr. De La Cruz for most of his life, I agreed to represent Hay-SOOS DE La Cruz. I believe he is completely innocent of the charges against him. He has no prior arrests and has a record of service in Father Javier's parish."

"I've completed a review of Mr. De La Cruz's background. It shows no prior arrests or problems with the law. The charges are serious. However, I also agree with the prosecution. Based on what was presented by both sides, bail in granted. Bail is set at $29,000 cash surety bond. This hearing is over. Court date is set for 30 days from today."

Mr. Allen glanced at me angrily, then turned to Mr. Chavez. In a harsh voice, he said, "See you in court. This kid is going down!" And he left the room.

I looked at Mr. Chavez with a slight smile. "Does this mean I can go home?"

"Hay-SOOS, the judge granted you bail, but there has to be $29,000 dollars put in a surety bond before you can go home."

In desperation I looked to Father for help. "Now what happens?"

"You have to stay locked up until the money is raised."

"I'm never getting out of jail."

"It's going to take a real miracle to raise that kind of money."

Mr. Chavez looked at Father, "We have to trust God."

"Hay-SOOS, you need to start praying really hard tonight," Father Javier said.

"I will."

The marshal grabbed me by the arm and walked me back to the van. As the two were walking out to their cars, Father Javier told Robert, "You handle the legality and let me handle the money. God just gave me an idea on how to raise the money. On Sunday we have three Masses with over 1,500 people attending each Mass. During the announcements, I am going to share what Hay-SOOS is facing. Most everyone knows him as my head altar boy. I am going to ask for a special offering for him."

"Is that legal?"

"It's God's money and Hay-SOOS is one of God's children. The Bible says, 'If God be for you, who can be against you?'"

"I can't argue with God. It's one thing to get bail another to prove his innocence. Let me know how it goes, Father."

"I will."

     Pastor Eric Sanchez

The court hearing was on a Friday morning. I was brought back to the jail and taken to my cell. I threw myself on the bed and cried for hours. I had given up hope. There was no way my grandma could ever come up with that kind of money. I felt completely helpless. All of a sudden, out of the corner of my eye, I had a vision of my aunt Sister Rosa standing in the cell. She was smiling at me. "Hay-SOOS, remember the story of the staircase? How all the sisters of the convent prayed a novena to St. Joseph, the patron saint of workers? We are praying a novena to St. Anthony, who is the patron saint of miracles. God knows you need one now. God is with you. Don't give up hope."

My thoughts went back to the time my aunt Sister Rosa shared with me the miracle of the staircase. Reflecting on the story, I had a peace come over me and again had hope. I started to pray for God to intervene.

On that Sunday, Father Javier did what he said he would do. He called for a special offering for Hay-SOOS from the congregation. Father was so excited; he couldn't wait to call Robert to give him the good news. He called him at home on Sunday afternoon.

"Robert, this is Father Javier. Get the papers in order tomorrow for Judge Gray. Hay-SOOS is going home. We received $32,000 in the offering Sunday for Hay-SOOS."

"That is a miracle."

"God is in the miracle business."

"That's $3,000 more than we need. Robert, I felt God would want to bless you with it."

"God is good all the time. I'll take care of the paperwork first thing Monday and meet you at the jail. I want to see Hay-SOOS' face when you tell him what God has done."

Monday morning came around with the same routine. Rattling at the front door, which meant breakfast was being served. Tired and exhausted from worry, I grabbed the tray. I was looking at one egg, over easy, with hash brown potatoes and one slice of burnt toast. At least the coffee was lukewarm, not cold like it normally is.

As I ate breakfast, I wondered what today would bring. I was coming to grips with the reality that I was going to stay here until I go to trial. Not a good thing! Hours had passed when one of the guards came to the door to tell me that my attorney was in the visitation room, wanting to see me. I was shackled and taken to the visitation room.

There sat Mr. Chavez and Father Javier. Mr. Chavez had papers in his hand. Father looked at me with a smile and said, "Hay-SOOS, today is a day that the Lord has made. Rejoice and be glad in it."

I just looked at him with somewhat of a smile and said, "Good morning, Father."

Father looked at me and said, "God has answered your prayers. You can go home today."

I was overtaken with joy as Mr. Chavez ordered the guard to unshackle me. I was given back my clothes and belongings. On the way home, Father said, "This is going to be a surprise for your grandma. She doesn't know about you getting bail. You can tell her how God did a miracle."

"How did God do it?"

Father just looked at me with a smile and said, "Just thank God and give Him the glory."

CHAPTER SIX

THE NEXT FOUR WEEKS

We drove past the rectory and up the driveway to our small house. I jumped out of the car and ran into the house looking for grandma. She was cooking tamales in the kitchen. As that heavenly aroma filled my head, I yelled out, "What's for dinner?" She turned in shock, threw her arms around me, hugging me.

"My Hay-SOOS! How did you get out of jail?"

Just then she glanced at the kitchen door and saw Father standing there. With tears in his eyes, he said, "This truly is a miracle!"

My grandma looked up with her hands raised and thanked God. "Come, sit. Let me fix you some tamales. I just made some red chile. I hope it's not too hot."

We all sat and ate. I shared with them how bad the jail food was and how I had given up hope. I shared about the vision I had of Sister Rosa appearing in my cell. "Mama Luz, Hay-SOOS' court date is set for four weeks from today. We're going to need a bigger miracle for that. We need to start praying that Hay-SOOS is found innocent of the charges against him." Father thanked Mama Luz for dinner, hugged me, and left.

I had four weeks before my court date. Somehow, I felt in my heart that these four weeks could be the last days of freedom for me, so I decided to live my life like it was before this whole thing happened. I started working on a bike I had been making for a friend of mine. On Sunday I served Mass with Father Javier. I had so many people come up to me after Mass to say hello and tell me that they were praying for me. I would thank them with a smile and a hug. On other Sundays, more people would come up after Mass to talk with me and say they were praying for me. Sometimes I couldn't hold back the tears, I was so touched. Most of my friends still spoke to me and hung out with me. Others wouldn't have anything to do with me. I now knew who my real friends were.

Things hadn't changed. I still stayed up to help Grandma with the cooking and took tamales and biscochitos to the plaza the next morning to sell. Some of the people who would normally buy from me just ignored me. I had no idea why, and for the first time, I came home with a few dozen tamales. I told Grandma about being ignored, she would say to me, "Don't worry, Hay-SOOS. It's not your fault. Any food that is not sold, we will give to the homeless shelter." I found out later that I had made the headlines in the Santa Fe newspaper. Now I was an accused rapist and an outcast.

The Sunday before my trial date, Father Javier asked me to stay after Mass. He said he had something to share with me. We walked across the street to a nice restaurant. We sat at the back table for privacy. As we were eating and enjoying our food, Father asked me about the past three weeks.

"It's not been good," I told him. "Some of my friends and people at the plaza who normally buy grandma's tamales stay away from me. I picked up a newspaper off a bench at the plaza. I was the headline on the front page, 'Local youth accused of raping a 12-year-old child.' I couldn't believe it."

Father shook his head and looked at me. "I am truly sorry to hear that. A few weeks ago, Mama Luz came to the rectory to talk to me. She was upset about a dream she had. She said that the dream took her back to the day that you were born. She said that at the time you were being born, a

     Pastor Eric Sanchez

vision came to her of Jesus being born in the manger. She said that you were born on the same day and around the time that Jesus was born. She said that you were born on Christmas Eve at 2:00 a.m. She heard the voice of your mother Rosa speaking to her, saying, 'Mom, take care of my son. Raise him knowing God and loving God. Watch over him and keep him safe so God can use him some day to do good.'

Your grandma can't understand why God is letting this happen to you. She feels that she raised you the way your mother wanted. She feels like she let your mother down. She also told me that an audible voice spoke to her and said, 'Go light ten candles and pray for Hay-SOOS.' She started to light the candles when she realized she had left her purse at home and had no money. Just then a bright light shined through a stain glass window and there appeared a maiden in a veil who gave her ten coins to light ten candles. When Mama Luz turned around to thank the woman, she had disappeared. She asked me what I thought and what it all meant."

"What did you tell her?!"

"I held her hand and said, 'Mama Luz, you are a good and godly woman and you have not failed your Rosa. You have raised Hay-SOOS to know, to love, and serve God. God tells us in His word that His thoughts are not your thoughts, neither are His ways your ways. Everything that has happened to Hay-SOOS these past few weeks is for a reason. All things work for good to them that love God, to them who are called according to his purpose. God knows Hay-SOOS didn't commit that crime. I have always believed that Hay-SOOS was a special kind of boy from the time I had him in my catechism class. I hoped that someday he would take the vows of poverty and chastity as a Jesuit Franciscan priest, but now I think God may have other plans for Hay-SOOS.'

"Mama Luz looked at me with a smile as she wiped the tears from her eyes and said, 'Let God's will be done in my grandson's life.' She hugged me and thanked me for having me in your life and walked off.

"Hay-SOOS, this may or may not give you comfort right now, but I needed to share it with you. Whatever happens in the court room next week, guilty or not, accept it as part of God's plan for your life. Remember what God said, 'I will never leave you nor forsake you.' I have something for you, it's my personal Bible. I received it when I was ordained and I want you to have it. Read it every day. Psalm 23 is my favorite psalm."

"Father, I'm afraid of what might happen in court. I have this dark cloud of fear lingering over me. My life will be over if I go to prison. How do you serve God in prison? I wish I had never been born!"

Father said, "Hay-SOOS, don't say that. Focus on the good and trust God. There were times when I wanted to give up being a priest. I didn't think I could live up to my vows of poverty and chastity. It was because I seldom read the Bible. The more I read, the stronger my faith became. God speaks to us through His Word. God took me to Psalm 34. That nailed it for me. I never questioned my calling again. Don't let the devil use fear against you. Just do it!"

"I'll do my best. Just pray for me, Father. Pray hard."

Father laid his hands on me and prayed over me. As he was praying, I felt the dark cloud of fear lift off of me. After he prayed, I embraced him and thanked him for sharing with me. We left the restaurant and went our separate ways.

CHAPTER SEVEN

JURY TRIAL

The thing that I feared the most had come on me, my trial date. That morning Father Javier and Robert Chavez came to the house early. They were there to prep me. I had to dress in a suit and tie. Grandma looked at me for the first time in a suit and tie. "You look so handsome, Hay-SOOS."

I asked her, "Are you coming to the trial?"

"No," she replied. "I am going to stay and pray for you, hijo mio."

Driving to the court house, Robert said to me, "Stay between us as we enter the court house."

"Why?" I asked him.

"We drove by the court house before coming here. There were news and TV media and crowds of people lined up waiting for us to show up. There were protesters. Some had signs supporting you and others calling for the death penalty. We want you to be safe. This is not going to be good. The news people have blown this way out of proportion. This is Santa Fe County's first child rape trail."

It was just as they had said. News and TV people surrounded us as we drove up. People were yelling at me, "CHILD RAPIST!" and held signs saying, "DEATH TO CHILD RAPISTS!" I kept my head down and walked between Robert and Father into the court room. We were seated on one side of the judge, and the state prosecuting attorney, Jack Allen (whom I was told by Father was an atheist), sat on the other side of the judge. Off to the right of the judge is where the jury of five women and five men would be seated. Seated behind me were a few of my friends, all the priests from the rectory, other altar boys who served Mass with me, parishioners, and most of the teachers and nuns from Loretto Academy. I had a lot of support.

On the other side sitting behind the prosecuting attorney sat the family, friends and others who supported the victim. The court room was full, and people outside watched on closed circuit TV screens.

People started to enter until all the seats were filled. The jurors entered and were seated. We all rose as Judge Gray entered the court room. The Judge asked the prosecuting attorney to proceed. The first person to testify was a man who claimed to be at the park the day of the incident. He claimed to have witnessed a man raping and attempting to kill a child. When asked if that man was in the court room, he pointed to me.

I immediately turned to my attorney and said, "He is lying, there wasn't anyone else in the park. Just ask the two police officers. Because he's claiming to have been in the park that day, he must be the one who raped the girl and is trying to put the blame on me."

The two police officers were called to the stand to testify what they had seen. Both stated that I was standing over the girl. They said that I was trying to get their attention to come help the girl. They claimed that I was acting as if I was helping her. They didn't see me actually rape the girl, but since they saw no one else around, they assumed it had to be me. The prosecuting attorney approached the bench to tell the judge that the parents of the child gave permission for their daughter to testify on her own behalf. The judge said that it is highly irregular but would allow it. The girl was called to the stand. The attorney asked her to describe in her own words what happened to her that day in the park. She gave a descriptive account of what happened to her; at the end, she showed the jurors the scar under

     Pastor Eric Sanchez

her chin where I supposedly tried to cut her throat. The attorney asked her if the man that did this to her was in the room. She pointed directly at me and said, "That is him." I knew by the look on the jurors' faces that I didn't have a chance of being acquitted. My attorney glanced at me, looked down, and shook his head.

The prosecuting attorney took up the morning session; four hours from 8:00 a.m. to 12 noon. Judge Gray called for court recess until 1:30 p.m., at which time the state defense attorney would proceed with his defense.

At 1:30 pm, court resumed. All stood as the judge entered the court room. The Judge then called on the defense attorney to proceed with his witnesses. My aunt, Sister Rosa, was the first to be called to the witness stand. Second was Father Javier. Third were teachers who knew me and taught me at the Academy in high school. Fourth were three altar boys who were friends and helped me serve Mass with Father Javier. The last witness was Bishop Ortiz, who had selected me and two other altar boys to serve the Christmas Midnight Mass in the Cathedral this past year.

Each witness was asked what their relationship was to me, how long they knew me, and if they ever knew me to be violent or use physical force with others. Who did I hang out with and where? What were my hobbies, my religious beliefs? What my thoughts were towards girls and if I had a girlfriend?

My attorney called the little girl to the stand and asked her if she was sure about me being the one who assaulted her, since she had testified earlier that her dress had been raised over her head. He asked her, "How could you see who it was that was touching and hurting you?" He then called each of the two arresting officers to the stand and questioned them about their presumption that because there was no one else in the park when they were questioning the girl that it had to be Hay-SOOS who committed the rape.

In his summation, my attorney turned to the jury and said that the person who testified against my client has perjured himself by the testimony of the two police officers saying there was no one else in the park when they were there. How could he point to Hay-SOOS and say he was an eye witness? Robert hoped he had established doubt in the minds of the jurors that the prosecution had not provided sufficient evidence nor proven beyond reasonable doubt that Hay-SOOS De La Cruz was guilty of all charges.

The judge gave the jury final instructions and dismissed them.

Four hours later, the jury came back in the court room. The judge asked them if they had reached a verdict. "Yes, your honor, we have." The foreman of the jury gave the judge the written verdict. I had to stand as the verdict was read. "On the charge of rape, we find the defendant guilty as charged. On the charge of attempted bodily harm, we find the defendant guilty as charged." My body went limp as I looked at Robert.

He looked at me with complete disappointment and said, "I am so sorry, Hay-SOOS."

I was immediately handcuffed and taken out the back door of the court room to a waiting van. Robert and Father Javier came with me. I asked Father Javier to tell Mama Luz I was sorry for all of this and to tell her I love her. I was driven back to the county jail.

My attorney and I were back in the court room three days later for my sentencing. The judge sentenced me to ten years, without parole, to be served at the New Mexico State Penitentiary. My attorney was very pleased with the verdict. He said, "Ten years is a slap on the wrist; these kinds of charges usually bring 23 years to life and sometimes a death sentence. The child's attorney and family were in shock that you only received ten years. They were very disappointed with the judge. They are trying to get the judge to reconsider and asking for a retrial. That will never happen. Just be thankful for the ten years."

CHAPTER EIGHT

PRISON TIME

At age 22, I entered the New Mexico State Penitentiary. Stepping off the bus with ten other inmates, we were taken to a holding room, which the guards jokingly called the reception center. I was strip-searched and given my prison clothes. I was given a bundle of blankets and later checked by the prison doctor. I was assigned to a cell with a 28-year-old black man named Jameer Cooper who claimed to be a Christian. He was anxious to know why I was here. At first, I was scared to death, but after talking with Jameer, who was soft spoken, I felt somewhat safe. I didn't share anything about myself. However, he was quick to share the many horrors of his childhood. After about 30 minutes of listening to him, I told him I just needed to rest for a few hours. He said, "You only have two hours before count time, so hit the sack. Lunch is around noon at the chow hall."

Sure enough, two hours later the siren sounded and everyone in the cell wing was standing in front of their cells. After count we were directed to the chow hall for lunch. As we entered the chow hall, 60 inmates were lined up to be served. The food was just as bad as it was at the county jail. After lunch we were taken outside for some sunshine and exercise, a jog around the track. We are given one hour of recreation time. After recreation we were taken back to our cell until dinnertime, which was around 5:00 p.m.

Back in our cell, I found Jameer to be a bit stand-offish. I asked him why. He said, "Hay-SOOS, you need to know about prison life. You are a Chicano." I asked him what that meant.

"It's slang for a Hispanic or Latin person."

"I am Hispanic, so what?"

"So, you need to eat and hang with other Hispanics. I hang with my own kind, blacks."

"So, is that why you wouldn't sit with me at lunch or work out with me outside?"

"Yes."

"If you claim to be a Christian, you know God does not look at you as black or me as Hispanic. We are all the same to God."

"That's true, but that's not the way it works in prison. Most of the blacks in here are Moslems. I am one of the few Christians in our group. We look at blacks as brothers, no matter what we believe. I've been here over seven years. If it wasn't for my brothers, I would be dead by now. The white supremacy guys are the ones you need to watch out for. They hate everyone. They will kill you if they get the chance. Now tell me why you are in prison. What is your crime of choice?"

"I have not committed any crime. I don't want to talk about it right now."

"Hay-SOOS, was it that bad that you don't want to talk about it? I'm getting the picture now. You should have been put in one of the dormitories, but for some reason, they brought you to this cellblock. This is a much safer place to be. You only get to come to this cellblock by requesting a transfer out of a dormitory for your own protection. Only two classes of inmates come to this cellblock, snitches and child molesters or pedophiles. I requested a transfer into this cellblock because a brother tipped me off that one of the new guards put the word out that I was snitching on them.

"Hay-SOOS, never talk to the guards or try to become friendly with any of them. They are not your friends. Sometimes they will single out the weaker inmates for information. They will tell you that if you don't tell them what they want to know, they will put a 'snitch jacket' on you. You don't want that, it's a death sentence.

"The cowboy that put a snitch jacket on me was Officer Fuentes. His nickname is 'Green Eyes.' He is trying to make a name for himself. He's a new correction officer, a hard-nosed, strictly by the book guy. He is physically abusive towards the inmates, especially pedophiles. Just watch out for him. If I am wrong about you, Hay-SOOS, I'm sorry, but you are too new of an inmate to be a snitch. The only other class is child molester. Is that why you're here?"

"I was falsely convicted. I never molested that little girl."

"Really? That's what they all say. But if you say so, Hay-SOOS, I'm inclined to believe you. I won't say a word about this to anyone."

Just then the bell rang for 5:00 p.m. dinner.

The next morning, the bell rang for breakfast. After going through the chow line, I looked around to find some Hispanic guys. Off in a corner was a table with some Hispanics sitting together. I walked over and sat down with them. One looked at me and said, "Who in the hell are you and why are you sitting here?"

"My name is Hay-SOOS."

"Well, Hay-SOOS, who invited you to sit with us?"

"No one."

"That's right, Vato. So, go sit somewhere else. You're not welcome here."

"Why can't I sit here? I was told that I should sit with my own kind."

"Do we look like your kind?"

"You are Hispanic, right?"

"What are you, some kind of stupid? We are Chicanos."

Just then the older guy sitting at the back of the table said, "Enough! Can't you see he's a new guy? Hay-SOOS, come sit over here. I'm Salvador. Tell me, Hay-SOOS, how long have you been here?"

"Just two days. And you?"

"Me? I been here a very long time, I quit counting after 20 years. I don't normally do this, but something is telling me to bring you into our group. We old guys have seen what happens to you new young men. It's not pretty; you are considered 'new meat.' You hang with us and you'll be safe. We can protect you from other inmates but not from the guards, especially from 'Green Eyes.'" As he looked around the table, he asked, "Anyone have a problem with that?" No one raised their hand. I got the feeling that Salvador was the leader of the group and no one would dare go against him. I suppose that made me one of Salvador's boys.

Just then the siren for afternoon count sounded. Salvador leaned over to me and said, "See you in the yard. Look for us at the south gate next to the weight equipment." I said, "Ok." and thanked him for making me part of the group.

After count I eagerly rushed out to the yard looking for Salvador. Sure enough, there they were, pumping weights. They had their shirts off. Never saw so many tattoos on arms, stomachs, and backs. I said to myself, "They don't look like me." I just kept my shirt on and just sat with Salvador as we watched the guys pumping weights.

One of the officers took note of me being with Salvador. He moseyed over and asked Salvador, "What's up with the new guy?"

Salvador said, "He's with us now."

"That's a good thing because some of the others are checking him out. They want to hit on him. Just thought I'd let you know."

"Thanks for the heads-up, officer."

After the officer moseyed away, Salvador leaned over and told me, "That is Officer Fuentes. He's the one we call 'Green Eyes.' He's been here for a short time. He could care less about any inmates' well-being. He hates inmates, especially child molesters. He enjoys physically abusing them. He has eyes on you for some reason. He is setting you up for something. Just be careful with him. Do not get caught alone with him. He'll hurt you."

Salvador asked me if I had a job yet. I said, "No, I didn't know you could work or had to work in prison."

					Pastor Eric Sanchez

"You need to if you want to buy stuff. Nothing is free in this place."

"I like working."

"What kind of work can you do?"

"Well, I can repair and build bikes."

"Would you like to apply for a job in the maintenance department?"

"Sure."

"I'll see what I can do." Just then the siren came on, ending recreation time. It was time for afternoon count, then back into our cell.

Back in the cell, Jameer and I were able to talk and share about our day. I shared with him all about what happened with Salvador, meeting up with Officer Fuentes, and the warning Salvador gave me about Officer Fuentes who they called "Green Eyes." I also told him that I might be working in the maintenance department. Jameer was glad that I had a good day but said, "Not all days are going to be like today."

As the days turned into months I got settled in with the group. They were starting to like and talk with me more. I let my hair grow long and grew a beard. I was talked into getting tattoos on my arms. I would get one every week or so. Somehow, I felt empowered and different with tattoos. I felt like I fit in more with the group. Thanks to Salvador, I did get the job working in the maintenance department and was drawing a weekly paycheck. It was enough to buy all the stuff I needed.

It was three months before Father Javier came to visit me. I shared with him everything that had happened to me since I came here. All he would say was how I had changed. I didn't look like the same Hay-SOOS. He said that my grandma had a stroke, was unable to speak or move her left side, and was bed-ridden in the hospital. I broke down in tears as Father proceeded to tell me how much she wanted to come and see me but could not bear to see me behind bars in prison.

"You know she loves you with all of her heart."

"I know she does. I just pray that God will take her home and not let her suffer."

"Hay-SOOS, I talk to her as if she can hear me."

"Tell her how much I love her and that I think about her every day and that I am doing well."

"I will, Hay-SOOS." As Father was leaving, he said, "I'll try to come see you more often."

CHAPTER NINE

SIX MONTHS LATER

I got the job in the maintenance building and worked alongside of Salvador who was the foreman. One day, Officer Fuentes walked into the maintenance building asking for Salvador. He told Salvador that he needed a worker to go with him to one of the stairwells to fix a railing. He asked specifically for me. Salvador, looking suspicious, called me over and said that I was to go with Officer Fuentes to fix a railing and that I needed to be shackled. I found it strange that he was by himself. There are always two guards that escorted you from one place to another.

After being shackled, I left with Green Eyes as he escorted me to cell block one. As we entered, I noticed that the building was empty. He walked me over to the stairwell where the railing was broken. As we were standing at the top, looking down the stairwell, he pushed me. I tumbled head over heels all the way down the stairwell. When I hit the bottom, I just laid there, bruised, with pain in my right hip. Officer Fuentes immediately came rushing down the steps, yelling, "Are you alright? You must have tripped over something." I looked up at him thinking to myself, "You know you tripped me and pushed me." He immediately was on the radio calling for help.

Two other officers and a medical technician rushed to see how badly I was hurt. They took me to the hospital unit where I was examined and x-rayed. I had some head trauma along with some bruises and a pelvic fracture. They put me on narcotics for the pain, which diminished it somewhat.

The next day, the prison physician wanted to talk with me about surgery. I told him I didn't want to have any surgery. "If it is a fracture, I'll be alright in a few weeks." I was in the hospital for three weeks, healing. I had to go through some physical therapy for another three months. I still had some pain, and when I walked, it was with a slight limp. I felt that the limp would slowly go away after a while. I was wrong. It didn't.

When Jameer and Salvador found out what had happened to me, both knew it was not an accident. They both wanted me to file a complaint against Officer Fuentes. When Fuentes learned that I was thinking about filing a complaint against him, he threatened to put a snitch jacket on me. I knew what that meant, a death sentence. I backed off from filing.

Weeks turned into months and I was able to go back to work. It just wasn't the same. Salvador and some of the guys in the gang were upset with me for not filing a report on Officer Fuentes, while others were feeling bad for me. What really riled me was that Officer Fuentes would occasionally come by the shop to see how I was doing. With a smirk on his face, he would say, "Glad you're doing better." I found out later that I was not the only inmate who had been physically abused by Officer Fuentes. He had abused one of the white supremacy guys and was jumped by three of them in retaliation and was beaten up. Those three guys got seven days in "the belly of the beast," and an additional five years each to their sentences for attacking an officer. The belly of the beast is an isolation cell; a dark, 10'x10' room with no toilet and no water sink and no windows. You get three glasses of water and one sandwich a day.

Being in prison for four years felt like ten years. Jameer and I would have long talks about life in general. I broke down one night and told him that I just couldn't take it anymore. He said, "I know exactly how you feel.

I felt the same way a few years ago. I was looking for a way out. I came really close to hanging myself. The day that I was going to do it, a man came to my cell asking if I needed prayer. He introduced himself as a Christian volunteer. I said, 'That's nice, this is the first time someone like you has come to this cellblock.' He said he'd been coming to this prison for the past two years."

'I hold a Bible study every Thursday in the chapel but never come into cellblocks. I feel the LORD led me here for a reason, so here I am. Can I pray for you?' I said, 'Why not? I need all the help I can get. I'm not a religious guy.'

"He said, 'Neither am I.' And so, he prayed for me and asked if he could leave me a Bible. I said, 'Sure.' He slipped a Bible under the door. I knew that all this was not by coincidence. I started reading the Bible every night. For some reason, I started reading in the gospel of John. When I finished reading, I knelt down in this cell and gave my life over to God. Since then I've been attending His Bible study every Thursday night.

"Hay-SOOS, you need God in your life! Come with me tonight to the Bible study. It's non-denominational. You'll enjoy it, they have Christian music. There are always 30 to 40 inmates that come. You can bring that Bible you never read and use as a pillow."

"Jameer, I have God in my life. You know that I was an altar boy, ask Father Javier."

"That does not make you born again."

"What do you mean by born again?"

"Read the Gospel of John, chapter 3, verse 5. Jesus tells you that you need to be born again in order to see the kingdom of God. Hay-SOOS, just come with me to the Bible study tonight, ok?"

"All right, all right, I'll come. But I am still going to stay a Catholic,"

"Fine, see you at 8:00 in the Chapel. You won't regret it."

I had to work late that night but got off early enough to attend the Bible study. There were quite a few inmates signing in. As I entered the chapel, I felt a peace come over me. There was a boom box playing songs about

Jesus. Some of the inmates were standing with their arms raised and singing. The volunteer came over to greet me.

He said, "My name is Renee Duran. You must be Hay-SOOS. Welcome to the Bible study." I asked him how he got my name. He said, "Jameer was here earlier to tell me that he could not make the Bible study tonight and that you would be coming. I am so glad that you made it. Have a seat. We will be starting in a few minutes."

As I sat and listened to the songs, a lot of the inmates came over to welcome me. Renee turned up the volume of the boom box and all the inmates stood and started singing along with the songs that were being played. I loved the guitar-playing and singing. It lasted 30 minutes. It was a new experience for me. I didn't want it to stop. As the pastor slowly turned down the volume, he let everyone sit quietly for a few minutes to meditate with God.

He started the Bible study. "Good evening. I see we have quite a few new guys here tonight. For those who don't know me, my name is Renee Duran. I am a volunteer Bible teacher from True Hope Covenant Church. I want to thank you for coming tonight." The pastor had us turn to the Gospel of John. He talked about the Divinity of Jesus, that He is the Light of the World; that to whoever receives Him, to them He gave the power to become sons of God. He said that God the Father and Jesus are the same. He said that John 10:30 tells us that. I always thought of Jesus as the Son of God, not God the Father. In John 10:30 Jesus said, "I and the Father are one."

An hour had passed, and as he closed, he asked the new inmates if they wanted to ask Jesus into their heart. Some raised their hand; I was not one of them. However, I really enjoyed the Bible study. I couldn't wait to get to my cell to share with Jameer about what happened in the Bible study.

Jameer was up when I got back to the cell. "Well, Hay-SOOS, how did you like the Bible study? Did you meet Pastor Renee?"

"I did. He was very nice. The Bible study was very different from the Masses I've served in."

     Pastor Eric Sanchez

"Hay-SOOS, it's not a Mass! It's a Bible study."

"Yes, I know that now. I felt like God was speaking to me the whole time I was there. Father Javier gave me his Bible years ago. He said if I read it every day that it would bring me peace and direction. I was so wrong in not doing that. I asked God to forgive me and to give me direction in the next five years that I have left to serve. I am going to continue attending Pastor Renee's Bible study. There is so much more I want to know about God and Jesus. I also want to talk to the Chaplain about serving in the Chapel. My purpose for the next five years is to serve God wherever He needs me and to draw near to Him and Jesus by reading my Bible. Pastor Renee said our only true hope is in Christ Jesus. I believe he is right."

I remembered what Father Javier once said to me, that one day can change the rest of your life. What happened to me on that day at the park changed the rest of my life for the worst. The day that I went to the Bible study changed my whole outlook and direction for the rest of my life for good. I had that desire again to want to serve God. God showed me how I could serve Him here and now in this prison.

CHAPTER TEN

THE CHAPLAIN

It's amazing how God makes things happen. I had wanted to make an appointment to see the Chaplain but was afraid to confront him. I had this fear that he would say to me, "I don't need any more Chaplain's helpers right now." But then I came to work one day, and Salvador called me over to tell me that a request came in for some work to be done in the Chaplain's office. The order was for some bookshelves to be built. I was given the order to do the work. I could not believe it. God not only opened the door to see the Chaplain but to work building bookshelves in his office.

The next day, I showed up for work and met the Chaplain. He was sitting at his desk looking at some files. He got up and asked if I was the one who was going to build the bookshelves. I said, "Yes, my name is Hay-SOOS."

"Hello, Hay-SOOS. I'm Chaplain Ray. It's nice to know you. I'll be in and out of the office. If you need me for any reason come and get me. I'll be in the chapel."

"Sure thing, Chaplain."

The chapel was right next to the Chaplain's office. There was a window looking into the chapel from the Chaplain's office, so I could see into the chapel. I started building one of the bookshelves. The shelves turned out to be several wrought iron pieces that needed to be put together, not wood shelves. The Chaplain kept coming in and out of the office and noticed that I was having a hard time putting the pieces together. He finally came over and asked me how things were going.

"Not too well, Chaplain. There's no instruction sheet to this wrought iron shelves kit."

He came over to see if he could help me figure out how to build it. He and I spent the afternoon trying to build the first shelf. During that afternoon, the Chaplain started asking questions about me. I told him my story. I also told him how I wanted to talk to him about serving as a Chaplain's helper but had a fear of being rejected and how God opened the door for me to be here.

"Hay-SOOS, it's not a coincidence that you're here. I've been praying for someone to apply for that position. I've had to let my assistant go. I was getting too many complaints from some of the non-Christian volunteers. Do you know that the Chaplain's helper needs to cater not just to Christians but to other religious leaders and volunteers?"

"Oh, no, I didn't know that, Chaplain."

"Do you have a problem with that, Hay-SOOS?"

"No. If God put it on my heart to be a helper, it's not a problem with me, Chaplain."

That afternoon I filled out an application for the position of Chaplain's helper. The Chaplain said that I would need to give up my job with the maintenance department and that he would call and make that arrangement for me. I wasn't sure how this would affect my relationship with Salvador and the group. I knew that God would work it out. The Chaplain and I bonded as he helped me finish putting the bookshelves together.

     Pastor Eric Sanchez

CHAPTER ELEVEN

FOUR YEARS LATER

I continued to attend Pastor Renee's Bible study every Thursday night and eventually gave my life over to Christ.

What took place over the past four years was sad and a blessing at the same time. My best friend and mentor, Father Javier, was diagnosed with cancer, and with chemotherapy, he was able to fight the cancer off for three years. In his last letter to me, he said that he was ready to go home and be with the Lord. He was giving up the fight. As we wrote back and forth, he became aware of how much I had read the Bible. In my last letter to him, I reminded him of what the preacher said in the book of Ecclesiastes, "To everything there is a season and a time to every purpose under heaven: a time to be born, and a time to die." I told him how much I loved him and was going to miss him. I thanked him for being in my life.

In the letter, I reminded him of the time when he asked if ever I thought of becoming a priest and that I had said that I was not good enough to be one. "Well, Father, I have become a priest since I have given my life to Christ. 1 Peter 2:9 says, that I am a chosen generation, a royal priesthood. I thank God for your Divine Calling. I am sure that you have many rewards waiting for you in heaven. We will have eternity together with Christ. I hope you are able to read this letter before God takes you home. Love, Hay-SOOS."

The Chaplain called me into his office one day to tell me that he had read in the Santa Fe News obituary column that a Lucia De La Cruz known as Mama Luz had passed away at the age of 92. He wanted to know if that was my grandmother who had raised me. I told him that had to be my grandmother but never knew her as Lucia. I broke down and cried, saddened and upset because I was unable to attend her funeral. I told the Chaplain that the first thing I was going to do when I get out is to go visit my grandmother's gravesite, to tell her how much I loved her, to thank her for all she did for me and that I would see her once again in heaven.

Jameer, my cell mate, was transferred to another prison in Texas. He had been receiving letters from his sister whom he had never seen or met. He was excited to know that he did have a family who cared about him. She was married and had two children. She had been trying to locate Jameer for several years. She lives in Texas near Dallas. The children were excited to find out that they had an uncle and had also been writing to him. Jameer requested and got the transfer. I was so happy for him. He told me that we should try to stay in contact with each other. I never heard from him again. I prayed he is doing well.

My total focus over the past four and a half years had been serving God as a Chaplain's helper. I'd been blessed to know several Christian volunteers from different churches and had become friends with some of them. But I stayed true to Renee and his Bible study. He invited me to his church when I got out. He said that they have a program to help felons by providing housing and jobs. I had been praying for the Lord to open a door and lead me to a church that could help me with housing and some kind of a job. God is so faithful. He always seems to be one step ahead of me. I had six months left to serve of my ten-year sentence.

CHAPTER TWELVE

RELEASE

The day that I thought would never come was upon me. At 7:30 am on the day of my release, my cell door bolt was unlatched and the door unlocked. I gathered my belongings and was escorted by an officer to the reception area for my release. I was strip-searched and my belongings searched. The process was quick. The next thing I knew, the main door to the prison was opened and I was outside the prison gate in a whole new world. I was free at last. To my surprise, Pastor Renee, to whom I had been talking about their program to help felons with housing and a job, had someone waiting outside for me.

"Hay-SOOS, Renee sent me to pick you up. My name is Tomas and I'm with True Hope Covenant Church. I am the director at the Valencia House where you will be staying." He threw his arms around me and thanked God for my freedom. I fell to my knees and thanked God for saving me and keeping me safe all those years, even through the mental and physical abuse, which caused a permanent limp in my right leg.

"Tomas, it's a blessing to know you. Thanks for picking me up, I didn't know what I was going to do when I got out."

"I feel like I have known you all my life," Tomas said. "Renee has talked a lot about you over the past six months."

"Is the Valencia House in Santa Fe, Tomas?"

"Yes, it's just about six blocks east of the Cathedral."

As he was putting my belongings in the car, I asked him, "Where are you taking me?"

"Renee said that the first thing you wanted to do was to go visit your grandma's gravesite."

"How did Renee know that?"

"The Chaplain told Renee that since you were not able to attend your grandma's funeral, it was the first thing you were going to do when you got out."

Tomas drove me to the cemetery where my grandma was buried and I was able to pay my final respects to Mama Luz, my grandma who raised me. I will forever miss her, but I know that someday I will see her again in heaven. After I was able to spend some time at the gravesite, Tomas drove me to the Valencia House and showed me to my room. He told me to take a few days off to recover from the shock of being free again and that he would see me later. I asked him about Renee and when I would see him again. He said, "I don't know for sure, he will be in touch with you to see how you are."

A few days later, Renee did come by to see me.

"Hay-SOOS, have you had breakfast yet?"

"Not yet."

"Good, let's go. I'm buying."

As we were having breakfast, Renee pointed out that there was some work at the church that needed to be done and asked if I would be willing to work at the church. "It doesn't pay much, but it's a start." I told him that anything is better than nothing. As we finished breakfast, he drove me to the church. I was able to meet some of the guys on the cleaning crew. Their job was to keep the bathrooms, offices, and the main sanctuary vacuumed, the kind of work I did for the Chaplain in prison. I was free, happy, and again working for the LORD. After spending some time at the church, Renee drove me back to the Valencia House.

"Hay-SOOS, I'll pick you up at 7:30 to drive you to work, so be ready."

"Ok, Renee. Hey, thanks for everything you've done for me."

"It's just the beginning. God has a lot more in store for you. Just take it one day at a time. See you later, brother."

The next morning Renee was there right at 7:30 like he said. I was ready. On the way to the church, I asked Renee what time Sunday services were and if there were any mid-week Bible studies going on. He said that there are three services on Sunday: 8:00 a.m., 9:30, and 11:15 a.m. On Wednesday night, his friend holds a 7:00 p.m. Bible study that I can attend. What more could I ask for! I had a place to live, a job at the church, a Sunday service to go to, and a mid-week Bible study to attend. I was so excited to start living my new life! Thank you, Jesus!

Over the next two years, I focused on studying the Bible at night and working at the church, attending Sunday service and my mid-week Bible study. I met a lot of good and loving people and made a lot of friends.

One of the elders of the church was a man named John Vass. He was a very successful real estate agent who occasionally attended the mid-week Bible study. After Bible study one night, Mr. Vass asked me if I would be willing to do some office cleaning on the side. He said he was looking for a person to clean his offices. I said, "Yes, absolutely." So, I was hired to clean Mr. Vass' offices on the weekends.

Mr. Vass was drawn to me for some unknown reason and was always asking me about prison life and if I got my limp in prison. I shared with him my life's story, what happened to me in prison and how I got my limp. He always made time to listen to my prison stories as we were having lunch. During lunch we would talk for hours. He finally came out and shared with me that he had this recurring dream of being in prison someday.

I said, "Not you, boss. You're a godly man. You'll never be in prison. That's the devil trying to put fear in you and take your focus off of God and your duties at church. The Bible says, 'God has not given us a spirit of fear but of power, love and a sound mind.'"

"Wow! I never read that in the Bible. I hope that's all it is, Satan putting fear in my head."

I never thought that I would be counseling my boss. He was always open and listened to what I had to say.

CHAPTER THIRTEEN

THREE YEARS LATER

The next three years flew by faster than the previous two years. I still cleaned and maintained the main sanctuary at the church along with cleaning Mr. Vass' offices. I was now helping with the mid-week Bible study, sometimes teaching two times a month. I was able to move out of the Valencia house and afford my own apartment. I got back into fixing and rebuilding bikes for the kids around the neighborhood. I even got some of the kids to attend Bible studies. I was living a good life, happy and content with what God had blessed me with.

January 1977 - Three years before the Darkest Hour: "the prison riot"

One night after I had taught at our mid-week Bible study, a lady who had come to the study for the first time came over to talk with me. She wanted to talk with me in private. After everyone had left, she proceeded to share with me a dream she had about me. She said in her dream, I was speaking in front of a group of men. But what was strange about the dream was that all the men were wearing the same color of clothing. I asked her what color of clothing they were wearing. She said it was yellow. I stood in shock and was silent for a while. She asked if I was ok and I told her I was fine. She thanked me for the Bible study and left.

A feeling of darkness fell upon me like I hadn't felt in a long time. Thoughts of past prison experiences came to mind. Yellow was the color of the prison uniform I had worn for ten years. God knew that in my mind I had sworn that I would never ever enter into another prison, no matter what the circumstances. I was so troubled over what the lady had said to me but knew in my heart from knowing God's Word, that this could be a word of knowledge from God. I needed to seek confirmation from another person. I made an appointment with one of the counselors at the church to see what he would say to me.

MEETING WITH THE COUNSELOR

The day of my appointment, I walked into the counselor's office. "Good morning, counselor."

"Good morning, Hay-SOOS. How are you?"

"I'm not sure. That's why I came to talk to you."

"Ok, what seems to be troubling you?"

"You know that I sometimes teach the mid-week Bible study. Last week a lady whom I had never seen before attended the Bible study. After the Bible study, this lady wanted to talk with me. She proceeded to share with me a dream she had about me, that she saw me speaking to a large group of men, but the strange thing about the dream is that all the men were dressed in yellow clothing. Do you know that I served ten years in prison?"

"I didn't know that."

"Yes, it was ten years ago in prison that I gave my life over to the Lord, and for ten years, I wore a yellow prison uniform.

"The night that she came was the night I was teaching on 1 Corinthians 12, the lesson on spiritual gifts. In verse 8 it says that to one is given by the Spirit the word of wisdom; to another the word of knowledge by the same Spirit."

"Hay-SOOS, that is no coincidence, I do not believe in coincidence, I believe in the divine Word of God. I believe you were given a word of knowledge from one of God's messengers. She may have been an angel. God is speaking to you. I sense that God is telling you to go back into prison to teach His Word."

"But I swore that I would never ever go back into any prison again."

"Really, is that what you are telling God? Hay-SOOS, I believe there are two kinds of people, those who say, 'My will be done' and those who will say, 'Thy will be done.' Those who claim to be Christians and those who surrender and humbly seek His will. Only you can make the choice. Which one do you want to be?"

"I want to do His will."

"God's ways are not our ways, nor are God's thoughts our thoughts. He must have a good reason for sending you back into a prison. You should have a peace, not a fear about that. Satan will put fear in your mind to keep you from doing God's will."

"Thank you, sir. You gave me the confirmation I needed to hear. My life is not my own. I gave it over to the Lord years ago. His will be done in my life. All things work together for good for those who love God and are called according to his purpose. I do have a peace about this now. Thank you, Jesus."

CHAPTER FOURTEEN

BIBLE STUDY

After the session, the counselor prayed over me and I left feeling like a new chapter was about ready to start in my life. It took me two weeks before I got the nerve to call the chaplain at the prison to set up an appointment to speak with him. I prayed a lot before I went to see the chaplain. The Lord spoke to my spirit and said, "You are going as my ambassador. Blessed are the feet of those who bring good news."

As I entered the prison, just the sight and sounds of the doors closing and opening took me back to a life I never want to relive. Some inmates were wearing brown and some were in orange clothing and the general population was in yellow clothing. As I walked down the hall to the chaplain's office, I was escorted by a correctional officer. Inmates that passed me would say, "Good morning, sir," and I would answer back, "Good morning."

I entered the Chaplain's office saying, "Good morning, Chaplain. I'm Hay-SOOS."

"Good morning. I'm Chaplain Reyes. Have a seat. What can I do for you?"

"I came to talk to you about being a volunteer."

"What kind of volunteer?"

"I am a Christian and would like to come in to teach Bible studies."

"That's great. I am a Christian Chaplain."

"But Chaplain, you need to know a few things about me."

"Ok, so tell me."

I shared my whole life's story from the time I was falsely convicted to the present day. He sat there with his arms crossed and said, "That is one heck of a story. But I must say, I admire you for being faithful to what God has called you to do. We need more Christian volunteers in this prison. Only the Word of God can change these poor souls. First, let me tell you that you need to go through four hours of training and pass a background check. If you do that, then you can come into the prison as a volunteer."

"I can do that."

"Just fill out these forms and I will do the rest. It will be about 45 days before you can get on the volunteer list. Are you sure this is the prison you want to come into as a volunteer?"

"Yes, I am sure, Chaplain."

Forty-five days later, I received a call from the Chaplain telling me that I was put on the volunteer list and was now able to enter the prison. I had already put in the four hours of training and was waiting for the Chaplain's call. I was excited but still somewhat hesitant on what to expect in my first Bible study and being back in prison! I chose Friday night at 8 pm to do the Bible study in the chapel. I got clearance to bring in a CD cassette to play music. I was following the same format of the Bible study I went to when I was in prison. It was a blessing for me and I wanted it to be a blessing for those that came to my Bible study. I didn't know what to expect or how many inmates would come the first night. Should I give my testimony? What will I teach on? What songs should I play? I needed to stay within the rules that were given at the training session.

*

  Pastor Eric Sanchez

FIRST BIBLE STUDY IN PRISON

The Friday morning I was to have my first Bible study, I got a call from Renee, my friend, whose Bible study I attended while I was in prison.

"Good morning, Hay-SOOS, tonight's the big night! I thought that I would come and sit in if that's ok with you"

"Great! I'd love to have you come. Make sure you call to see if they are locked down."

"I'll do. See you tonight."

As Renee and I drove into the prison yard, we were stopped and Renee's vehicle was searched. After the search, we proceeded into the prison to check in. We were met by a corrections officer, who walked us back to the Catholic chapel. Inside the chapel, an inmate introduced himself as the Chaplain's helper. Steven was his name. He helped us set up chairs and the podium. As we were setting up, the inmates started to come in. They lined up to sign in for the Bible study. My mouth dropped when I saw over 25 inmates and all were dressed in yellow clothing! My thoughts went back to the woman's dream and my first Bible study years ago in this same chapel. After the inmates were seated, I took a few minutes to introduce myself.

"Hello, my name is Hay-SOOS. Thanks for coming. How are you doing? Where are you from?"

I shared that I had served ten years in this prison; how I gave my life to God in this same chapel. I was overjoyed with the number of inmates that had come and the few who came to the Lord that night. I was amazed at how they responded to the music and the teaching and how hungry they were for the Word of God.

I now knew why God brought me back to prison. I never felt such a love and compassion for anyone like God gave me for these inmates that night. I was already looking forward to the next week's Bible study. Renee even commented on how he felt a bonding and how anointed the Bible study was. I was on a "Holy Spirit high" when I left the prison.

CHAPTER FIFTEEN

ONE YEAR LATER

Weeks turned into months and months into another year. It was 1978, two years before the Darkest Hour (the prison riot).

The Bible study grew larger. Inmates stayed after the Bible study to ask me questions about the ten years I served. I was asked about my limp and if I was ever harassed or physically and mentally abused. I told them that I could not talk about any of my experiences. However, they started sharing their experiences with me and what was happening in the prison. I became a good listener.

Some inmates talked about how bad their living conditions were: the dormitories being over- crowded, their visiting rights being cut back, how bad the food was in the cafeteria, and some of their recreational time being taken away. The Bible tells us to be quick to listen and slow to speak. I was at a point where I didn't want to hear about their complaints. However, I felt the Holy Spirit prompting me to counsel them with the Word of God. I could sense the despair and hopelessness in their voices. These were the same feelings I had had years ago when I had given up hope.

There was a dark cloud of fear and unrest in the air and a feeling of hope-lessness similar to what I had felt years ago when I was in this place. I felt a demonic spirit hovering over the prison. The inmates were frightened because hardcore inmates who had been in solitary confinement were now being placed in minimum security dorms. Dorms that were built to house 90 inmates were now housing 125 inmates. Some of the inmates were now sleeping on mats on the floor. The Chaplain's helper, Stephen, was telling me that this prison was built to house 900 inmates and there were now 1,157 inmates being housed in this facility. Because of the shortage of correction officers, the captains and lieutenants were working overtime in order to make up for the shortage. They also had to sit in on the volunteers' activities.

"Hay-SOOS, don't tell anyone what I just shared with you. This comes direct from the Chaplain. He shares a lot with me that maybe he shouldn't."

"So that's why I have a captain or lieutenant monitoring my Bible studies. I thought it was because of the number of inmates who attended."

"No, it's because of the shortage of C.O's."

In one of my Bible studies, there was a Captain who sat in for the service. It happened to be communion night. As the inmates were signing in and I was setting up the communion tray and grape juice, the Captain came over to me and asked if he could take communion with us. He said he was a Christian and loved the Lord. I told him it would be a blessing to the inmates and to me if he did. That was a first for me.

A few Bible studies later, the same thing happened. However, this time a Lieutenant came in to monitor the Bible study. This time the Lieutenant was not so nice. He stayed at the door as the inmates signed in. He didn't even acknowledge me. I asked Stephen, "Who's the Lieutenant?"

He said, "It is Lieutenant Fuentes."

"Oh," I said. "Not very sociable, is he?" The name didn't ring a bell at first. During the Bible study, the Lieutenant just glared at me. He even cut the Bible study short for no reason at all. This upset the inmates and me. He left, not saying a word to me or to any of the inmates.

It had been several months since my boss, John Vass, had called or spoken with me. I wanted to share with him how the Bible study was going in the prison. I knew he would be excited to hear how well it was doing.

A week later, on Sunday when I was cleaning his office, I heard the front door open and close. It was Mr. Vass.

"Mr. Vass, what are you doing? It's Sunday. You never work on Sunday."

"Hay-SOOS, how are you? I'm sorry I haven't been in touch. It's been crazy around here lately."

"No problem. I figured you were busy. Business must be good!"

"Yes, business is great. I just closed on a large ranch for Judge Gray, north of Red River."

"Judge Gerald Gray?"

"Yes, Judge Gerald Gray. How do you know him?"

"Judge Gray was the judge who granted me bail and sentenced me to serve ten years at the New Mexico State Penitentiary."

"Judge Gray is a God-fearing man and attends our church. Didn't you know that?"

"No, I didn't know that. I have never seen him in church."

"He's retired and up in age. He normally attends Saturday night service and you go to the Sunday 11:00 a.m. service. That's why you have never seen him at church. Listen, Hay-SOOS. I can't talk now, but I will call you for lunch next week and we can catch up on everything, like your Bible study. I have something to share with you also. By the way, I get a lot of compliments on how nice the offices look. Thanks for your hard work."

I never heard from Mr. Vass that following week when he said he would call me. I knew he was very busy, so I just told myself that he would call me the first chance he got.

CHAPTER SIXTEEN

THREE WEEKS LATER

I received a call from Renee asking if I had heard about John Vass. "No," I said. "The last time I saw and spoke with Mr. Vass was in his office three weeks ago. Why?"

"He was arrested a few days ago."

"Arrested? You're kidding!"

"I wish I was. He was having lunch with Pastor Drake. After lunch he was taking a short cut to his car through an alley when he heard a young girl screaming. Two men were assaulting her. He jumped in and fought with them but was knocked unconscious. When he regained consciousness, there were two Santa Fe officers standing over him and the young girl had been raped and killed. He was charged with the rape and murder of the girl. That's not the worst of it. The young girl was Juanita Fuentes, the daughter of Karen Fuentes."

"Who is Karen Fuentes?"

"Karen Fuentes attends our church and leads the women's Bible study on Wednesday morning. Sarah Vass is her assistant. Sarah is John Vass' wife. They are the best of friends and have been leading that Bible study for the past three years. Over 100 ladies attend every Wednesday morning."

"Oh, my God! This is unreal! Who told you all this?"

"Pastor Drake was allowed to visit John in jail. This is John's version of what took place."

After hearing all of this, the only thing that came to mind was the recurring dream that John shared with me over lunch. He dreamt that he was in prison and a fear gripped him every time he had this dream. Now it had come to pass! Maybe God was trying to tell him something! I had told him that it was Satan who was putting that fear in him. I suppose I was the one who was wrong because the fear had become very real for him.

Months later John was tried and convicted. He was sentenced to 27 years to life for the rape and murder of Juanita Fuentes. The sentence was to be served at the New Mexico State Penitentiary, just south of Santa Fe.

One Friday night, the Chaplain called me into his office before my Bible study. He was concerned about the tension and mood among the inmate population. He said that all correctional officers and prison staff were briefed about a possible takeover of the prison by inmates. "It's my responsibility to inform all the volunteers," he said. "That is why I am telling you. The second thing I want to share with you is what happened to Lieutenant Fuentes' daughter." He said that the Lieutenant was in his office when he got the call from his wife about his daughter being raped and killed. The Chaplain wanted me to ask our brothers in Christ to pray for the Lieutenant because he was taking the death of his daughter really hard. He was also blaming God for his loss. "Along with the briefing of the possible takeover, we now have an inmate who has been accused and found guilty of the rape and murder of the daughter of one of our own correctional officers. And this inmate will be serving his sentence in this prison. I am afraid of what Lieutenant Fuentes might do to John Vass."

"Chaplain, you know that Lieutenant Fuentes is despised by all the inmates because of his emotional and physical abuse of the inmates. I'm not sure how they will take my asking them to pray for him."

"Hay-SOOS, do you remember what Jesus said to Peter in Matthew's gospel?"

     Pastor Eric Sanchez

"Sorry, Chaplain. I don't remember, not off hand."

"Does seventy times seven ring a bell?"

"Oh, forgiveness. Was it when Peter asked the Lord how often he should forgive his brother?"

I was reminded of what Jesus said to Peter in Matthew chapter 18 verses 21 and 22 about forgiveness.

"Chaplain, you just told me what my lesson will be tonight."

That scripture cut me to my bone. I needed to forgive Fuentes. I had carried hatred for him over all these years. I finally put it all together. Karen was Juan Fuentes' wife and Juanita was their daughter.

Now I realized that Lieutenant Fuentes is Juan Fuentes, the same guard who physically and mentally abused me 15 years ago; the same one who pushed me down the stairwell causing my broken hip and my permanent limp. He didn't look the same. The 20 years of being a prison guard had taken its toll on him physically and mentally.

I will never understand how God allows circumstances and events to shape our life. As Christians we know that all things work together for good to them that love God, to them who are called according to His purpose.

I could see how God had been working in my own life by bringing me back into prison to start a Bible study and giving me a love and compassion for men that I despised. This was his purpose for my life. It's a beautiful thing to know what God's will is for your life. I was saved in prison, but I couldn't understand how God would allow a godly man like John Vass to be falsely accused of rape and murder and sentenced to 27 years to life in prison. John was a deacon in the church and his wife was involved in the women's ministry. In my spirit, I was questioning God on this one! What came to mind was what Father Javier once told me when I was questioning God's hand on my life, that "My thoughts are not your thoughts, neither are your ways my ways, says the Lord. For as the heavens are higher than the earth, so are my thoughts than your thoughts." Who was I to question God's plan for John's life?

I questioned the event that happened in the Fuentes family, feeling somewhat sorry for Juan Fuentes after knowing that his little nine-year-old sister was molested by a family member and that she had taken her own life shortly after she was molested. I didn't understand how Juan Fuentes could carry a hatred and resentment towards God because of what happened to his little sister and blaming God for it. How could a man have so much hatred toward God, while having a wife and two kids who were God-loving and saved, and his wife conducting Bible studies and bringing other women to Christ? Are the sins of the father handed down to his family? I don't know. I hope not. I was anxious to see God's hand in all of this.

After a short leave of absence, Lieutenant Fuentes returned to the penitentiary to resume his duties. A few days after the Lieutenant returned, he called the Chaplain to have coffee with him. They always had their cup of coffee every morning before they started their daily duties. This had been going on for several years. The Chaplain was the only friend that the Lieutenant had in the entire prison.

Before the next Bible study, I was able to get back with the Chaplain to tell him that most of the Christian inmates had been praying for Lieutenant Fuentes. "Well, Hay-SOOS," the Chaplain said, "you can tell them that God has answered their prayers." The chaplain began to share with me about Lieutenant Fuentes and his change of attitude towards God.

The Chaplain asked me if I had ever doubted God's Word. I said, "To be truthful with you, Chaplain, yes, sometimes. Why do you ask?"

"Well, I have, too, at times. All the years that the Lieutenant and I have known each other, I have always shared Jesus with him. He would say to me, 'Chaplain, if we are going to be friends, let's have an understanding to agree to disagree on our spiritual beliefs. I get enough of this Jesus stuff at home from my wife and kids.'"

"Ok, fair enough. Every once in a while, I would throw in some short scripture about God's love. But the Bible tells us in Isaiah 55:10-11, 'As the rain cometh down, and the snow from heaven, so shall my word be that goes forth out of my mouth: it shall not return unto me void. It will accomplish what I desire and achieve the purpose for which I sent it.' Only God knows what it will take to bring a person to repentance."

CHAPTER SEVENTEEN

REPENTANCE

The Chaplain continued to share with me what happened one morning over coffee. "The day the Lieutenant came to speak to me in my office he was a broken man, broken in a good sense. He was a changed man."

Lieutenant Fuentes shared with the Chaplain that the day he received the call from his wife about Juanita, his daughter, was the day they were having coffee in the Chaplain's office. He said, "I am responsible for my daughter's death. I was supposed to pick her up from school that afternoon and I totally forgot. If I had been there to pick her up like I should have, she would still be alive. My wife never said a word to me about that. Instead, she threw her arms around me and held me tight as we both held each other, crying and sobbing. I was blaming and cursing God for my daughter's death. I felt that God was punishing me for not being the godly husband and father my wife wanted me to be in the family.

"One night I couldn't hold in my anger any longer and unloaded on my wife. I asked her, 'Why do you serve your Christian God who allowed our daughter to be raped and killed? What kind of God is he? And how can you still be friends with the wife of the person who raped and killed Juanita?'

When I finished unloading on her, she quietly wiped her tears from her eyes and said, 'I am hurting just as much as you are. I don't know why God allows bad things to happen to his children. Let me be honest with you, my love. When I was told that she was found raped and killed and who it was that was accused of the charges, I was more enraged with you for not going to pick her up like you were supposed to have done. I know Mr. Vass. He is not capable of such a crime. The spirit of hatred came upon me, something that I have never felt before. I could not let this anger and hatred which is sin be in me if I truly have the Holy Spirit in me. It is God's love and grace that gives me the ability to forgive.'

"So now you are taking sides with the person who killed our daughter. He is going to pay for what he did. Twenty-seven years to life is not enough punishment in my book. His life is in my hands now. I am going to put him in general population at the prison the first chance I get and let the word out about his crime. Inmates despise child killers and rapists.

"She begged me not to do that. She said that she couldn't live with the thought of her husband taking the life of an innocent person, someone whom she thought was falsely accused.

"She told me, 'If you ever want to see your daughter and your little sister again, you must repent of the anger and resentment you have towards God and ask Him to forgive you. The Bible tells us that if we confess our sins, He is faithful and righteous to forgive us our sins and to cleanse us from all unrighteousness. All these years you have carried anger for God that should be towards Satan. The Bible tells us that the thief comes only to steal and kill, and destroy, but that Jesus came that we might have life and might have it abundantly.'

"My wife said that God loves me in spite of my anger at Him. This is the first time I have ever listened to her lecture me on religion. What she said made sense. That night in my office I fell to my knees and asked God to forgive me of all my sins. I also asked Him if my little sister and Juanita are with Him in heaven. I never got an answer from Him but had an overwhelming peace come over me, a peace I had never felt before, I took that to mean that His answer was, "Yes."

The Chaplain responded, "Juan, the minute you walked into my office, I felt I was looking at a new man, that Jesus describes as being "Born Again."

"That's exactly how I feel, Chaplain, like I have been reborn."

"HAY-SOOS," the Chaplain told me, "we are brothers in Christ. You needed to hear all of this, so we never again question God's way of doing things. He is never late or wrong in His methods."

"You're right, Chaplain. However, I need to see fruit in the Lieutenant life's before I can accept him being born again. I pray God gives me the strength and grace to forgive Lieutenant Fuentes for what he did to me. I can only do it in God's time and through His love."

"Amen to that, brother."

I thanked the chaplain for sharing with me and left his office shaking my head as the Lord reminded me that he is not a respecter of persons and what he said in John 3:8 "The wind blows where it wishes and you hear the sound of it but do not know where it comes from and where it is going; so is everyone who is born of the spirit."

CHAPTER EIGHTEEN

SIX MONTHS BEFORE THE RIOT

The Bible study continued to grow with many inmates coming to Christ. I always had a correctional officer present to monitor the Bible study. Sometimes it would be a Captain, but never again did Lieutenant Fuentes monitor the study. I would get some positive feedback from the inmates about the Lieutenant, that he had mellowed out somewhat. He was not so rough with the inmates and had sometimes actually spoken to them.

One Friday night before the Bible study, I felt a spirit of heaviness come over me as I was praying. I was praying for John Vass and Lieutenant Fuentes. I was asking the Lord to comfort the families as they live out the rest of their lives without their loved ones. I prayed for Sarah Vass, who lost her husband John to an accusation of the rape and killing of Juanita Fuentes, and was serving a life sentence in prison. I also prayed for Karen Fuentes whose 15-year-old daughter was raped and killed. I mourned for the families as though I was feeling their pain. I started to recite Isaiah 61:3 "…to appoint to those who mourn in Zion, to give to them a garland for ashes, the oil of joy for mourning, the garment of praise for the spirit of heaviness."

That night at the Bible study, we were having communion. It was Lieutenant Fuentes who showed up to monitor the study. Just before the inmates came in to sign up, and as I was setting up the elements, the Lieutenant came over to speak with me. I was hesitant and kept my distance. He shared with me that he had accepted Jesus as his Savior and said that he was so sorry for what he had done to me years ago. He asked me if I would forgive him for causing me so much pain. His eyes were full of tears as he spoke in a broken voice; my eyes started to tear up as well. We both embraced each other as I said to him in my broken voice, "I do forgive you, in Jesus' name." That night was a work of God. We all took Holy Communion together, the inmates, the Lieutenant, and me. It was the most anointed Bible study I have ever had.

CHAPTER NINETEEN

LIFE CHANGING

John Vass entered the New Mexico State Penitentiary to serve his sentence; four months before the darkest hour, the riot.

A bus with new inmates arrived at the prison with a new inmate by the name of John Vass. Inmate Vass was charged with the rape and killing of a 15-year-old girl by the name of Juanita Fuentes. She was the daughter of Lieutenant Juan Fuentes, a guard at the New Mexico State Penitentiary. Inmate Vass was to be put in cell block three. Cell block three is a maximum-security unit. It is used for protective segregation. Protective custody includes inmates who are considered informants and inmates suspected to be child killers or child molesters. However, cell block three was full to capacity, so inmate Vass was reassigned to dormitory E- 2, a medium security unit in the South Wing of the penitentiary.

Two weeks later, inmate Vass requested an appointment with the Chaplain. Inmate Vass was taken to the Chaplain's office with his hands and feet shackled.

"Good morning, Chaplain. My name is John Vass."

"Hi, John. I'm Chaplain Robert. What is it you wanted to see me about?"

"I have been here two weeks now and have not had anyone come to see me and have not been able to use the phone in the dormitory to make any calls. I know my wife is wondering what is going on."

"I'm sorry, John. The administration has changed a lot of rules over the past few weeks, such as cutting back on visitation hours and on calls going out and coming into the prison. Your wife needs to call the prison and ask to be put on the visitation list. There is a form she needs to fill out before she can come in to visit you. That's the same for anyone who you want to see and visit you. They must be on that list."

"Is that something you can do for me, Chaplain; call my wife and tell her how to get on the visitation list? I would want my pastor and some business associates also on that list. Did you know that I am a deacon in my church?"

"No, I didn't know that. What church?"

"True Hope Covenant Church."

"True Hope Covenant Church, I have a volunteer from that church who comes in on Friday nights and does a Bible study in the chapel. He does a great job and is respected by the inmates. He has quite an attendance. He served ten years in this institution 16 years ago. You should try to attend his Bible study sometime. I'm not allowed to have contact with inmate families. I can talk to the volunteer from your church to see what he can do. Give me your wife's name and phone number and I will ask him to talk to your pastor. Your pastor will be the one to handle this for you."

"Oh, thank you, Chaplain, and God bless you. By the way, who is the volunteer that does the Bible study?"

"His name is Hay-SOOS."

"De La Cruz?"

"Yes, De La Cruz. You know him?"

"Yes, I do. I hired him three years ago to clean my office buildings in Santa Fe. He has been a blessing to me and to the church. He does a lot for the church."

"It truly is a small world, John. It will all work out. The guards are here to take you back to your dorm."

   Pastor Eric Sanchez

On the way back to the dorm, John started thinking, "Should I start attending Hay-SOOS' Bible study? I'm a deacon and he is just a volunteer. Somehow, I felt inadequate going to his Bible study. I haven't been to many Bible studies the whole time I have been at True Hope Covenant Church. Deacons are the ones that do Bible study, not volunteers.

CHAPTER TWENTY

NEW LIGHT

Hay-SOOS must have followed through with Pastor Drake because John's first visitor was Pastor Drake. He came to see him two weeks later.

John asked the pastor why his wife hadn't come to see him. Pastor Drake sadly said, "Give her some time. She is not ready to come see you behind bars."

"How are Sarah and the kids holding up?"

"Not good, John. Not good. Sarah is thinking of quitting the women's ministry over this whole incident. She thinks that Karen Fuentes is going to ask her to step down from the women's ministry because of what has happened. I keep telling her that the Fuentes family does not hold the Vass family responsible for Juanita's death. We all know that John was falsely accused of the crime. I told Sarah that the Fuentes family is praying for all of you. This whole incident has been a tragedy and will be for the rest of your lives.

"John, I am reminded of what Billy Graham once said at one of his crusades: He said that God's love is just as real and just as powerful in the darkness as it is in the light. I want to know how you are holding up."

"Pastor, I don't know that I can do this. I feel like I am walking in the valley of the shadow of death like it says in Psalm 23. I know that I should fear no evil, but to be honest with you, Pastor, I am scared to death. I have been attending the Bible study that Hay-SOOS has on Friday nights. All I can say is that Hay-SOOS has given me a whole new light on the Bible. All this time that I have been going to church with my wife Sara, I thought that I had a relationship with God. I didn't. I was just playing church."

"John, I was not real sure about your relationship with God and in my way of thinking, you being a deacon in the church would surely have drawn you into a closer relationship with God. I now know I was wrong in asking you to come on as a deacon. I believe that it took this whole experience for you to become a child of God and be truly born again."

"Hay-SOOS shared with me how blessed I am to have the power of the Holy Spirit of God with me in the short time that I have been in prison. He said that the first five years of his sentence was a living hell because he didn't come to the Lord until his sixth year of his sentence. I'm all in with God and my life is in his hands. I just need to ask God to take this fear away.

"There's just too much going on right now in this prison. It's ready to explode. This is hell on earth. I was first assigned to a protective custody unit for my own protection. However, there was no room, so they reassigned me to Dormitory E-2, a medium security unit. The dormitory conditions are horrible. There aren't enough bunk beds, so I slept on the floor on a mat. I had to cover my ears at night in order to sleep because the noise is so loud. Inmates are up all hours of the night making home-made liquor. During the day, there are at least 25 radios playing at the same time and all of them are on different stations.

"This place is a nightmare; no one feels safe in this place. The guards come around for morning and night count. At night they sometimes don't even do count. They are too afraid to come into the dormitory for fear of stepping on some of the inmates sleeping on the floor and causing a disturbance. Dormitory E-2 should only house 65 inmates. There are over 120 inmates being housed in this dorm right now.

    Pastor Eric Sanchez

"I was told by other inmates that weeks ago the administration allowed maximum security convicts, the hardcore, to come into this dormitory because their cell block was being renovated. They have taken over this dormitory. One inmate told me that most of the inmates are now submissive to their every command. One inmate said he has requested to be transferred to another dorm and that 30 or more inmates have requested transfers to other dormitories over the past three weeks.

"I try not to mingle too much with other inmates, but I overheard that some of the white supremacy group inmates were planning a disturbance and the possibility of a hostage-takeover. Pastor, tell Sara and the kids that I love them and that I have given my life over to God. I am being transferred to cell block four, which is a maximum-security unit. It's a protective segregation for those who are considered snitches, child killers, or child molesters. I don't want Sara to know that I am in this cellblock. She would not be able to handle knowing that I am in here. If anything happens in this prison like a takeover or riot, cell block four is the safest place to be in."

"John, we are all praying that God keep you safe and will intervene in your case and reveal the real person who raped and killed Juanita. Just be patient and keep drawing closer to God."

"I will, Pastor. Thanks for coming to see me, and may God bless you. I look forward to Friday night Bible study now. That's the only true hope I have now to have some peace in my life. Hay-SOOS is a great teacher and the worship is outstanding."

CHAPTER TWENTY-ONE

TAKEOVER

My last Bible study was before the riot on Friday, February 1st and Saturday, February 2nd 1980.

"Hello, this is Hay-SOOS De La Cruz. I am a religious volunteer and I have a Bible study tonight at 7 pm. I was just calling to see if you were locked down."

"Not at the moment. We are not locked down, but I need to tell you that a few volunteers are not coming in tonight. They somehow got word that there might be a lockdown later in the evening."

"Well, if they're not locked down, I will be coming in for Bible study. Thanks for the heads-up."

On my drive to the prison, I was unsure as to what lesson I was going to teach. All of a sudden, all of the thoughts of my life started flashing before me, all the good things and all the bad things. There was a voice speaking to my spirit, saying, "The Spirit of the Lord is upon you because He has anointed you to preach the Gospel to the poor and set free those who are downtrodden. For I was naked, and you clothed me; I was sick, and you visited me; I was in prison, and you came to me. Truly I say to you, to the extent that you did it to one of these brothers of mine, even the least of them, you did it to me. Yet you do not know what your life will be like to-morrow. You are just a vapor that appears for a little while and then vanishes away. Well done, good and faithful servant. Come be with me on my glorious throne."

I couldn't speak or think. Was the Holy Spirit telling me that my life was coming to an end? At the same time, I had an overwhelming joy in my spirit. I sang songs of praise the rest of the way to the prison.

On my way to the chapel, I saw that the Chaplain was still in his office. I went in to say hello and asked him why he was working late. He said that for some reason he needed to stay and pray for the prison inmates and staff. I asked him why. He told me he had a dream the other night about the prison being taken over by the inmates and some of the staff taken hostage. "I pray that it was just a bad dream, so I will be here praying most of the night."

"Chaplain, if you are still here after Bible study, I will join you in prayer. The Lord spoke to my spirit on my drive to the prison. I'll share with you what was said to me. I have to run because I'm late for Bible study. I'll talk to you later."

As I entered the chapel, my helper had already set up the pulpit and the communion elements', the grape juice and bread wafers. He said that we were going to have a full house tonight and that Lieutenant Fuentes was in earlier wanting to talk to me. The Lieutenant said he would be back later to monitor the Bible study.

Stephen, my helper, was correct. We had over 75 inmates in attendance. Worship was strong and the Holy Spirit came down on the service like I had never felt before as we were having communion. After communion one of the inmates stood up and gave us a word of knowledge: a reading from Revelation Chapter 2, verse 8; the message to the church of Smyrna. He read: "And to the angel of the church in Smyrna write: The first and the last, who was dead and has come to life says this: 'I know your tribulation and your poverty (but you are rich). And the blasphemy by those who say they are Jews and are a synagogue of Satan.

                    Pastor Eric Sanchez

'Do not fear what you are about to suffer. Behold, the devil is about to cast some of you into prison, that you may be tested, and you will have tribulation ten days. Be faithful until death, and I will give you the crown of life.

'He who has an ear, let him hear what the Spirit says to the churches. He who overcomes shall not be hurt by the second death.'"

The inmate said, "Thus says the Lord," and sat down.

Still another inmate stood up and gave another word of knowledge by reading all of Psalm 91. It seemed as though the Lord was telling us what was going to happen in the prison. Shortly after the last word of knowledge was given, the prison alarm went off and the prison went into lockdown. The inmates were rushed off to their dormitories for count. Lieutenant Fuentes took charge and led the inmates out of the chapel and back to their designated cells.

Being short of guards that night, the Lieutenant had to help with the inmate night count. He was responsible to help with the count in all of the dormitories, along with monitoring some of the volunteer activities. He decided to monitor my Bible study since he had had a born again experience a few weeks before. The Lieutenant and two other officers went to dormitory E-2 to start their night count. E-2 was considered a dangerous dormitory because of the inmates who were brought there from a maximum-security unit. Renovation of that cell block had forced their removal into E-2. It is customary to isolate and disperse dangerous individuals throughout the medium security living units when maximum security units are not available. But most of the dangerous inmates in cell block five were transferred to dormitory E-2.

I was ordered to go down the corridor to the officer's mess hall and wait for the lockdown to be lifted. The Chaplain was there having coffee. He looked at me with a smile and said, "Don't worry, Hay-SOOS. We'll be out of here in a few hours. No one can leave the prison when a lockdown is in place."

Lieutenant Fuentes and one other staff officer, a shift supervisor, were doing the inmate count in E-2. The procedure for securing E-2 was that the staff member would gather at the door to the dorm and keys were given to him. He would then unlock the door, open it, and allow the other officers to enter the dormitory. Then the door would be shut and locked. Some inmates say that sometimes the door is not locked but is left open about six to eight inches. This is to help the two officers inside with a quick escape in the event that some inmates try to overpower them and take over the dormitory. On this night, the cell block door was left open six to eight inches and not locked.

As Lieutenant Fuentes and the other officer entered, the Lieutenant went down the right aisle and the other officer the left. They were both four to five bunks into the dormitory when one inmate leaped from the bed and hit the still open door. He was quickly joined by other inmates. Lieutenant and the other officer were jumped at the same time. They both were quickly overpowered. Lieutenant Fuentes had the size to offer a challenge, but the other officer was short, middle aged of only average physical fitness for his age. Upon being overpowered, they were then stripped, bound, and blindfolded.

One of the inmates stripped Lieutenant Fuentes of his uniform and dressed himself in it. He then led other inmates down the stairs and through the unlocked gate. They ran north along the corridor and then proceeded to take four more hostages and unlock the other dormitories, releasing more inmates. They were moving in the direction of the control center when they ran into the officers' mess hall where the Chaplain and I were waiting out the lockdown. But it had now turned into a full-blown prison riot. We were both taken hostage along with other correction officers who were there having coffee. The chaplain and I did not offer resistance, but a few officers tried to resist and were stabbed, beaten, and finally subdued.

The inmates took the chaplain and myself to E-2 day room where Lieutenant Fuentes and others guards were being held. Some of the officers who were able to free themselves ran into the day room of dormitory F-2 where they were protected by sympathetic inmates. Some inmates then

   Pastor Eric Sanchez

took the keys from the guards and unlocked the doors to other dormitories to release other inmates. Within minutes more than 500 inmates were freed and had access to all the dormitories.

One corrections officer was blindfolded and then dragged downstairs to the main corridor by a belt looped around his neck. He was pushed and kicked northward down the hallway toward the Control Center. In the Control Center, one of the guards manning the Control Center heard an inmate's voice on the two-way radio saying that the shift captain had been taken hostage. The voice demanded a meeting with the Governor, representatives of the news media, and the Secretary of Corrections.

From inside the Control Center, the guards could see a group of 75 to 100 inmates gather in front of the glass windows in the main corridor. One of the inmates demanded that the grills be opened, allowing the inmates' access to the Control Center. When that did not happen, the inmates began to beat one of the hostages with steel rods and pipe, telling the Control Center officer he could expect the same treatment if he did not cooperate. The inmates began to beat on the Control Center windows with pipes and canister-type fire extinguishers. After several blows, the window began cracking. Minutes later inmates were in the Control Center of the penitentiary.

The inmates now had control of all the keys to all of the cell blocks and started to release all of the maximum-security convicts. The residents of cell block three were all released. Many of the inmates broke into the hospital and pharmacy and a variety of drugs were consumed, along with paint thinner and glue. With the help of keys from the Control Center, inmates obtained a heavy-duty acetylene cutting torch stored in the plumbing shop in the basement under the kitchen. Now they could use this torch to cut through the corridor grill to enter into cell block four.

Cell block four was labeled by most other inmates as an informant or snitch cell block, and other inmates, such as child rapists and pedophiles, were placed there for other protective reasons. Prisoners in cell block four had listened and waited for hours as the inmates took over the prison, thinking that they would be safe in their cell since the inmates could not find the right keys to unlock their cells. They were unaware of the acetylene cutting torch that the inmates had acquired.

Just after dawn, rampaging inmates who were shouting, "Kill the snitches!" finally cut through the cell block four grill with the acetylene torch and gained access to the protective custody inmates. Those cutting into the cellblock shouted the names of their intended victims waiting inside. Groups of violent inmates, described as "execution squads," went from cell to cell in the protective custody unit designating their victims, while waiting for a cutting crew to torch open the panel used to unlock the cells. Some impatient killers threw flammable liquids into locked cells and onto inmates marked for destruction and then ignited them.

When the execution squad came to John Vass' cell, they were unsure as to who he was. John cried out, "I am not a snitch! I am in this prison falsely accused of a crime I did not commit! Please don't kill me! I have a wife and two kids and I am a deacon in my church. I'll do anything you want! Please don't kill me!"

One of the squad inmates said, "This is new meat. I want this guy for myself. Take him to where the other hostages are." So, as they took John out, some of the squad inmates started to molest him, but the squad leader told them to lay off. "He's mine!" he cried. John was taken to where the other hostages were. There was Lieutenant Fuentes, Hay-SOOS, and the Chaplain, along with other guards. All of them had been beaten and roughed up, except for the Chaplain. The plan of the leaders of the white supremacists was to use the Chaplain as a bargaining chip; his life for the transfer of their top leader to other prisons and amnesty for the starting of the riot.

When the inmates came back from where the hostages were being held, they started to burn the bars of the cells with an acetylene torch to get to the inmates inside. When the cells were open, the rampaging inmates dragged out many of their cell block four victims and stabbed, tortured, bludgeoned, burned, hanged, and hacked them apart. Some of them were

 Pastor Eric Sanchez

thrown from upstairs tiers to the basement floor, where many of the bodies were found.

After the execution squads were done with cell blocks three and four, they proceeded to the E-2 day room where the hostages were being held. They were going to torture and slowly burn and hack Lieutenant Juan Fuentes for the physical abuse he inflicted on some of the white supremacy inmates, a slow death. John Vass was going to be gang-raped and then turned over to other inmates. They could do to him whatever they wanted. Because he was a volunteer, Hay-SOOS was going to be released as a gesture of good will.

As the execution squad inmates entered the day room, they proceeded to drag Lieutenant Fuentes out. However, the Lieutenant fought them off as best he could. The inmates started beating on him when all of a sudden, Hay-SOOS jumped on some of the inmates and started to defend the Lieutenant. He wrestled with them and was able to keep some of the inmates off of the Lieutenant. This infuriated the inmates and they started beating on Hay-SOOS. One of the inmates stopped them from beating on Hay-SOOS and said, "This is the Bible thumper. His name is Hay-SOOS De La Cruz. He thinks he is Jesus. Let's take him to the chapel and crucify him. We will nail him to the large wooden cross that's there." Hay-SOOS was dragged out of the E-2 day room and was taken down to the chapel, leaving Lieutenant Fuentes and John Vass for a later time. Hay-SOOS was taken to the chapel, where he was beaten to the extent that he was unrecognizable. He then was nailed to a large, old, wooden cross that had been donated and installed in the chapel years before.

Just as the execution squad inmates were heading back for Lieutenant Fuentes and John Vass, they were overtaken by the soldiers of the New Mexico National Guard and members of the New Mexico State Police, as they had finally taken back control of the prison.

CHAPTER TWENTY-TWO

THE AFTERMATH

Within five hours after the takeover of E-2, the rioting inmates had taken control of the entire penitentiary, had taken 12 hostages, and had begun to mutilate and kill fellow inmates. Thirty-three inmates were killed that night, including five inmates from cell block three, and 12 inmates from cell block four, the protective custody cell block.

Hundreds of inmates had broken out of the penitentiary to escape the riot. They surrendered to police and huddled in the yard along the perimeter fences. Blankets were the only shelter provided for the convicts in the yard.

Military personnel, volunteers, and professional medical personnel worked around the clock to treat and transport wounded inmates and correctional officers during the riot. Many of the riot casualties suffered life-threatening injuries, and all who received medical treatment survived.

From the very outset, prison officials discussed whether the prison should be stormed and recaptured. In considering whether to forcibly retake the prison, the calculation of potential hostage deaths was the deciding factor for prison officials. A forcible entry by police would have jeopardized the lives of the hostages.

On Friday night, when word got out that there was a riot at the New Mexico State Penitentiary, inmates' relatives started to arrive at the front gate of the prison. Family members were concerned about their loved ones inside the prison. There was much animosity and anger among the relatives toward prison officials because of the lack of information regarding whether their sons, fathers, or grandfathers were alive or dead. Some of the first to arrive at the prison were Karen Fuentes, the wife of Lieutenant Juan Fuentes, and his son Luke; and Sarah Vass, the wife of John Vass, his son, Matthew, and his daughter, Ruth. All of the real estate agents who worked for John were also there.

Pastor Neil Drake of True Hope Covenant church brought his prayer team and set up a prayer vigil for all of the inmates, guards and volunteers who were in the prison when the riot started. Many of Hay-SOOS' friends from Santa Fe, True Hope Covenant Church, and the Catholic parish joined the prayer vigil, praying that all would be safe. New Mexico District Court Judge Gerald Gray, a strong Christian who was responsible for sentencing many of the inmates serving time at the Penitentiary came to pray. He was a member of the church prayer team.

Robert Chavez, Hay-SOOS' and John Vass' defense attorney, was also at the front gate trying to get information from the warden's office and demanding answers as to who was being held hostage. Even Jack Allen, the prosecuting attorney and atheist, came to offer his services. He also demanded information from the Warden as to how he was going to handle restoring order to the prison.

At 1:30 pm on Sunday afternoon, the Northern New Mexico SWAT team and the Santa Fe Police SWAT team, along with some National Guard personnel, entered the prison and started taking over the facility. Later that afternoon, Jack Allen was able to get information from the warden; the list of names of 979 live inmates and hostages. Among the names were Lieutenant Juan Fuentes and John Vass. Another list of names was of the dead inmates. Among the names of the dead was Hay-SOOS De La Cruz, the volunteer who had been holding Bible studies for the past three years. He was found nailed to a wooden cross in the Protestant chapel.

There were 1,138 prisoners inside the prison at the time of the riot. On Saturday morning, many family members of prisoners were present at the front gate and along the outside fence, waiting for news regarding their loved ones.

True Hope manifested itself through faith in God in the darkest hours in the lives of the inmates, guards, and volunteers who were held captive and killed during the riot. Evangelist Billy Graham once said, "God's love is just as real and just as powerful in the darkness as it is in the light."

Jesus said:

> Greater love hath no man than this, that a man lay down his
> life for his friends.
>
> John 15:13

> **For God so loved the world, that he gave his only begotten
> Son, that whosoever believeth in him should not perish,
> but have EVERLASTING LIFE.**
>
> **John 3:16**

Lieutenant Juan Fuentes and John Vass are reminded every day that Jesus died on the cross for them. They are also reminded of what Hay-SOOS De La Cruz did in that prison on the night of the riot by saving their lives.

AFTERWORD

The following is taken from the Introduction of the Report of the Attorney General on the February 2nd and 3rd, 1980: Riot at the New Mexico State Penitentiary.

"Shortly before 2:00 a.m., Saturday, February 2nd, 1980, inmates at the Penitentiary of New Mexico near Santa Fe overpowered four correctional officers during a routine inspection in a medium security dormitory. The inmates rushed through the open dormitory door, and within minutes, captured four more officers. Using keys taken from the officers, inmates freed fellow prisoners of the southwest wing and then moved through an open grill gate to the administrative area of the institution, smashing their way into the main control center. With the seizure of the control center, the inmates gained access to every part of the main penitentiary building, where 1,157 male inmates were residing under the custody and care of 25 correctional employees.

"In the 36 hours that followed, 12 officers were held hostage, some of them beaten, stabbed, and sodomized. Thirty-three inmates died at the hands of their fellow prisoners, some of the victims tortured and their bodies mutilated. At least 90 other inmates were seriously injured in the riot, suffering from drug overdoses or from beatings, stabbing and rapes inflicted by other convicts. The majority of inmates had escaped to the outside of the walls by the time the riot was over.

"Prison officials communicated with inmates throughout the weekend in an effort to negotiate the release of the hostage officers and the surrender of the inmates. By 1:30 p.m., Sunday, February 3rd, 1980, the violence had spent itself; police and National Guardsmen retook the penitentiary without resistance. The State went about the business of identifying the dead and the living, providing temporary housing for the inmates, rebuilding the burned-out prison, preparing to prosecute criminal cases, defend civil suits, and if possible, learn what had gone wrong."

Pastor Eric Sanchez